A Vision of
the Aquarian Age

A Vision
of the
Aquarian Age

The Emerging Spiritual
World View

George Trevelyan

COVENTURE | LONDON

Published by Coventure Ltd., London 1977
Reprinted 1979
New edition 1984
Copyright © 1984 by Stillpoint Publishing

This book is manufactured in the United States of America.
It is designed by James F. Brisson, cover art by
William Giese and published by arrangement with
Stillpoint Publishing, Box 640, Meetinghouse Road,
Walpole, NH 03608.

ISBN 0-904576-52-3
0 9 8 7 6 5 4 3 2 1

Acknowledgments

For permission to use copyright material, the author gratefully makes the following acknowledgments:

Faber & Faber Ltd. for permission to quote from T.S. Eliot's "Little Gidding" and "East Coker."

Oxford University press, for permission to quote a passage from Christopher Fry's "A Sleep of Prisoners" and also D. H. Lawrence's poem "A song of a Man who has Come Through," the sonnet "Bodily Extension" by J. C. Earle and the poem "Eros Absconditus" by David Gascoyne.

The Estate of Robert Frost for permission to quote Robert Frost's poem "Trial by Existence."

Findhorn Press for permission to quote from Anthony Brooke's essay "The Awakening of Man" and also from David Spangler's "Revelation — the Birth of a New Age."

E. P. Dutton & Co. Inc. for a passage from R. M. Bucke's "Cosmic Consciousness."

Aurobindo Press, Pondicherry, for a passage from Sri Aurobindo's "The Future belongs to the Young" published in the journal "1."

William Collins Sons & Co. Ltd. for a quotation from Teilhard de Chardin's "Hymn of the Universe."

Geoffrey Chapman Ltd. for a quotation from Teilhard de Chardin in "Building the Earth."

Dr. E. F. Schumacher for a short passage from his book "Small is Beautiful."

Allen & Unwin Ltd. for permission to quote a passage from Bertrand Russell.

Contents

Foreword | by George Trevelyan

THIS BOOK is in no sense dogma to be believed. It is an attempt at exploration of Ideas which are alive and can therefore enter our consciousness and bring change. We can all recognize the faculty for apprehending an idea for its very beauty. We seize it out of the ether, with a feeling "that's lovely, that gives meaning to life." And then, all too often, the cold intellect comes in and says, "Oh, no you don't! You can't prove that and you must not accept what cannot be demonstrated to the senses." But we are exploring the *supersensible* worlds. The technique is to take these ideas (if we like them) and learn to live with them as if we believed, while at the same time reserving judgment and watching life in the light of them. Then there is no need for argument, that debased form of human exchange. Ideas of this sort are alive and will therefore draw to themselves a certainty as one lives with them.

A remarkable change is taking place in the intellectual climate of our time. The holistic world view is penetrating our consciousness and superceding the rational materialism which is surely proving inadequate to explain our fantastic universe. Really we are recovering what was called the Ageless Wisdom of the ancient Mysteries, which knew that the Universe is Mind not mechanism, that the Earth is a sentient creature and not just dead mineral, that the human being is in essence spiritual, a droplet of Divinity housed in the temple of the body. This vision, once apprehended, lifts the basic fear of death in our death-ridden culture. The body may be destroyed, but the soul/spirit in each of us is deathless and immortal.

Our age is filled with prophecies of doom and breakdown, which are obviously alarming. But the greater truth is that there is no death without rebirth, no renewal without the breaking down of outdated structures and habit patterns. Just because the world is so mad and so bad and so dangerous, it is valid to look at the apocalyptic picture. This suggests tht behind disaster is a transforming power at work out of the Living Whole, which can cleanse the planet, sweep away much that is negative and bring in a New Age. We certainly approach years of dramatic change. Technocratic man in greed, avarice and ignorance has failed lamentably in his stewardship of the planet and the Living Earth hits back at him in ever increasing disaster.

But the grasping of the holistic world view leads directly to the emergence of an alternative lifestyle, working with the Living Earth and not merely raping and polluting her. This means nothing less than the emergence of a new human species, filled with a love for all life and a readiness to serve the Whole in caring, cooperation and compassion. It has been called MULIER/HOMO NOETICUS — a human being balanced male-female, of developing consciousness. This may give meaning to the statement "the meek shall inherit the Earth," for behind NOETICUS is a divine power which in the long run is absolutely unconquerable.

Certainly the vision of the spiritual nature of man and the universe brings the conviction that the human potential is unlimited and that we stand at the threshold over which a quantum leap in consciousness is possible.

Cosmic consciousness, a blending of mind with Universal Mind, is being achieved and demonstrated by more and more people. This world picture by no means implies that we just sit back and let God do the job. Human initiative is the vital factor, but we are working with energies of life and being from the ocean of Divine Intelligence which can bring about change. There never was such a generation in which to be alive. "Look up, for your redemption draweth nigh."

12/19/83
[GLT/CMR]

I | A Spiritual World View

We LIVE AT PRESENT IN A time of trouble. Despite our dazzling technological achievements and our shrill claims of progress, affairs on "Spaceship Earth" are going very seriously wrong. Indeed, our problems have now assumed not local, not national, but planetary proportions. Perhaps there is some unknown factor we have forgotten. Perhaps there are certain basic questions which — amid the proliferating complexity of modern life — we find ourselves too busy or too harassed to ask. What our purpose might be on earth, for example. What life is about. Who we are. Why we are.

The present crisis should compel us to pause and consider, to reevaluate. It is obvious that unless we do so, there may well be grave consequences, and the very structure of our society and our economy will be faced with collapse.

We may well be at the end of an epoch of history. We may well be witnessing the breakdown of a civilization. After all, such things have occured before, and it would be naive to presume ourselves immune to the mishaps that befell the cultures of the past. But the very gravity of our situation renders consideration of the possibilities of rebirth all the more worth our while.

Many of us are already considering such possibilities. A remarkable phenomenon is occurring in our intellectual climate, a phenomenon that amounts to nothing less than a spiritual awakening. It is as if a fresh tide were rising in our consciousness, an inner flooding from some secret fountainhead, bringing with it a surge of new optimism. Those who discern or feel this energy find themselves linked by a sense of serenity and joy, a conviction that a new age is imminent. Paradoxically, it is with us already, working in human hearts, leavening our thinking, penetrating and suffusing our understanding.

The emerging world view is essentially simple. Grasping it requires no great intellectual effort, only a flexibility of thought, a readiness to delight in change, a resilience and youthfulness of attitude, regardless of how many years we may have lived.

A materialistic culture like our own might be described as outward-looking. It is preoccupied with facts and things, with the getting of more facts and things, with desires and their satisfaction. One tacit assumption of such a culture is that matter is the primary reality — if not, indeed, the only one. If there are spiritual values, these are not permitted to interfere with daily life. They are relegated to a safe periphery — music, literature, painting, conventional religious attitudes. These things, it is assumed, are to be studied, but not to be lived. Living should be concerned with "getting and spending," and with measurable quantities.

The spiritual world view stands in contrast to this position. It sees the world of Creative Spirit as primary — a realm of Absolute Being and Creative Intelligence, from which matter and the phenomenal or material world are derived. Understanding, in a spiritual world view, involves the capacity to look inward and so through into spheres of ever-widening consciousness. William Blake, that seer of the New Age, wrote that his task as teacher, artist and poet was:

> . . . to open the Eternal Worlds, to open the Immortal Eyes of Man, inwards, into the Worlds of Thought, into Eternity, ever expanding in the Bosom of God, the Human Imagination. (Jerusalem, Chapter I)

"Imagination," in Blake's definition of the word, is the faculty that opens in us the vision of the divinity in all living things and leads to higher knowledge and intuition. And it is imagination in this sense that is confirming in many minds today the reality of higher worlds, coalescing the vision and hope of a new society rising from our fragmented, chaotic and crumbling civilization.

The spiritual world view is a vision of wholeness, an apprehension of the essential unity of all life. Increasingly, our minds and hearts are recoiling from the concept that the universe is a mere dead mechanism of gaseous bodies turning through infinite aeons, with life but a chance accident for a brief span on this tiny planet. In more and more minds today, there is a deepening conviction that the whole is alive and is the work of Mind, of some Intelligence. Behind all outwardly manifested form is a timeless realm of absolute consciousness. It is the great Oneness underlying all the diversity, all the myriad forms of nature. It may be called God, or may be deemed beyond all naming — and therefore, as in the East, be called THAT. If one is of an agnostic turn of mind, one can refer to it as "creative intelligence." But from it derive all archetypal ideas which manifest in the phenomenal world. For that world issues ultimately from spirit, and its forms might be conceived as frozen spirit. The quality of Being permeates everything, suffuses everything. Divinity is therefore inherent everywhere. As Blake says, "Every rock is deluged with Deity." Or Gerard Manley Hopkins, "The world is charged with the grandeur of God." Or Pope, "All are but parts of one stupendous whole / Whose body nature is and God the Soul." Or Goethe, "All that is transitory is but a parable." The world of nature, in short, is but a reflection of the eternal world of Creative Imagining.

The inner core of man, that which in each of us might be called spirit, is a droplet of the divine source. As such, it is imperishable and eternal, for life cannot be extinguished. The outer sheath in which it manifests can, of course, wear out and be discarded; but to speak of death in relation to the true being and spirit of man is irrelevant. As Krishna says in the *Bhagavad Gita:*

> *The truly wise mourn neither the living nor the dead. There was never a time when I did not exist, nor you, nor any of these kings. Nor is there any future in which we shall cease to be. Bodies are said to die, but that which possesses the body is eternal.*

What then is the meaning of life upon the earth plane? We must recognize that there are many levels of being in which the soul of man may sojourn. The gravity field of earth is but the lowest plane, the darkest and densest theater of the drama. The soul belongs properly to higher and purer spheres. It incarnates for the purpose of acquiring experience in the density of earth matter — a necessary educational phase in its development. Such incarnation, of course, entails drastic limitation of a free spiritual being. Birth into a body is, in fact, more like the entry into a species of tomb. It is truly a kind of death, whereas release from the worn-out sheath of the body is a rebirth back into the subtler planes of wider consciousness from which we descend.

We must conceive of many levels of consciousness reaching back to the creative Godhead. "In my Father's house are many mansions," Jesus states in the New Testament. The Fall — as it appears both in the Bible and in the myths of all races throughout the world — may be regarded as symbolizing a descent into matter, an experience of separation from God with its attendant developments of pride and self-consciousness. When, like the Prodigal Son, man "comes to himself" and says "I will go back to my Father," the long return begins. He sets his pilgrim feet upon the path and, through the ages, must so cleanse his soul that it can move up to ever more refined planes of light.

Needless to say, I am using the word "soul" rather loosely to imply the imperishable entity in man. More precisely, we must recognize man as a threefold being of body, soul and *spirit*. The true individuality is spiritual in its nature. The immortal "I" is neither the soul nor the transient personality. In order to descend into the density of the phenomenal world, it must clothe itself, so to speak, in a protective sheath. Soul is the so-called "astral body" or "emotional body" which the eternal "I" draws about it, thus enabling it to experience one level of reality — that of the "soul" or "astral" plane. In like manner, from the great pool of etheric forces, the eternal "I" draws together the "etheric body," a network of vital forces which serve to hold together the particles and vortices of energy which comprise the physical body. These sheaths allow a spiritual being to function effectively on a given plane at a given time. But the personality, or lower ego, must not be identified with the eternal "I." In one of his poems, T.S. Eliot writes, "I said to my soul, 'Be still'." This statement suggests the real distinction between the eternal "I" and the soul vehicle.

When we speak of "higher worlds," we do not, of course, mean spatially distant. One should conceive rather of subtler planes interpenetrating denser ones. We all recognize that electromagnetic waves can pass through solid matter and remain invisible, unless we have instruments that can tune into them. In the same way, the higher worlds coexist with those we see around us. All levels interpenetrate, all levels are consubstantial. It is not a long journey in space to the higher worlds. On the contrary, the higher worlds have nothing to do with our conceptions of time and space. If one asks where the higher worlds are to be found, the only answer is: wherever the mind can direct itself to them. They are everywhere, but we must learn to tune in to a higher frequency-rate than that available to our five senses. Our senses are tuned to receive the vibrations of matter. They are thus the instruments by which we function in our earth-bodies. They may be conceived as filters which allow only a little of the life of the cosmos to penetrate the human consciousness. This is admirably expressed by Martin Armstrong's poem, "The Cage":

Man, afraid to be alive,
Shuts his soul in senses five
From fields of uncreated light
Into the crystal tower of sight
And from the roaring songs of space
Into the small flesh-carven place
Of the ear whose cave impounds
Only small and broken sounds,
And to his narrow sense of touch
From strength that held the stars in clutch,
And from the warm and ambrosial spice
Of flowers and fruits of paradise,
Into the frail and fitful power
Of scent and tasting, sweet and sour;
And toiling for a sordid wage
There in his self-created cage
Ah, how safely barred is he
From menace of Eternity.

To the filters of the five senses may be added the filter of conceptualization, of logical rational thought. If the universe is suffused with the creative power of Divine Mind, puny man in his evolving consciousness needs a filter to insulate himself against an overwhelming inrush of too great a pressure from the living cosmos. As T.S. Eliot says, "human kind cannot bear very much reality." The brain should thus be seen as an organ for reflecting and selecting ideas, enabling the intellect to function as an instrument within the limitations of matter.

The very convolutions of the brain may reflect, in fact, the convolutions of thought in the universe. In contrast, Mind implies that which can transcend brain-bound intellect and merge again with higher thought-worlds. As Rupert Brooke says, we are but "a pulse of the eternal mind." It was the colossal achievement of Rudolf Steiner (of whom we will speak further later) to demonstrate at the beginning of this century that, by intensifying his thinking and developing his latent faculties, man can achieve "sense-free thinking." This entails an elevation of thinking to merge with the "world process," thus offering the possibility of direct and immediate apprehension of truth and reality. For Steiner, in consequence, there were no grounds for claiming limits to knowledge. Indeed, Steiner's whole life was a demonstration that thinking, as he conceived it, was an instrument for exploring the creative thought of the universe and doing so not only in full consciousness, but with a certainty comparable to that afforded by scientific method. In this way, Steiner established the foundations for a true spiritual science. And his demonstration of "sense-free thinking" — as well as those of other modern adepts — destroys the primary argument against survival after physical death, namely that once the brain is gone there can be no individuality or consciousness. If man as a soul/spirit being is eternal, he is living in a different spiritual sphere when not incarnate in the body, and there a physical brain is obviously unnecessary. Thus it becomes apparent that consciousness widens when bodily limitations are transcended.

The concept of different levels of consciousness — of which earth is the lowest and densest — is basic to the world view we are considering. The spiritual being, Man, descends from a subtler plane to assume a body, the necessary sheath in which to live amid earth vibrations. This body is no more than a species of overcoat which may be discarded when worn out. We might also compare the body to a diving suit. If one wishes to explore the ocean floor, he may don a special suit which protects him from the immense pressure of the depths into which he will descend. Thus clad, held down by leaden boots, he may stump along and peer out through his visor into the marvels of the deep. And he may become so absorbed by those marvels that he forgets, for a time, the two tubes which — by providing him with oxygen — keep him alive and link him with the world above. If we, like undersea divers, break the surface and remove our helmets, we will breathe deep of sunlit air and recognize the atmosphere in which we properly belong. And should we choose to return to the depths, our entire attitude will be changed — though the significance and beauty of what lies below will in no way be diminished.

In short, then, there are subtler senses, undeveloped and often unrecognized faculties which can apprehend higher worlds. These can be perfected and trained through meditation and a variety of other techniques that serve to concentrate our energy and resources and distract us from distraction. Contact with the worlds of spiritual being is always possible and accessible if we can learn to overcome the sense of separation inevitably associated with incarnation, and if we can develop the dormant organs of perception. As Clarice Toyne says in *The Testament of Truth*, "Every cubic centimetre is shot through with all that is."

Thus it is with the spiritual world. If — in meditation or vision or true creative imagination — we begin to experience its reality, we will *know*, with indubitable certainty, that *it* is the realm to which we properly belong, and that we are only sojourning in the world of gravity for a brief period of education and experience. Once this recognition dawns, our whole attitude towards the body and the world will inevitably change. One will then see the soul as undergoing a form of allegorical pilgrimage, a journey of the kind so often symbolized in myth. It must submit to trials and ordeals, all of which are tests designed to train and strengthen it so that, when its course is run, it may return to the realms of light. And perhaps climb higher towards the Divine Source which was its origin and is its goal and ultimate home.

From this perspective, what occurs in life is not a sequence of chance mishaps, accidents and misfortunes, but a pattern that is, in some mysterious way, planned. From this perspective, it becomes apparent that our higher self has somehow chosen its own destiny, the destiny that we mistakenly ascribe to the transient personality. But this does not imply blind determination or predestination. The option of free choice is always available to the soul, but the flaws in personality — the soul's vestment — will draw it into situations, contacts and circumstances in which temptations will have to be confronted again and again, until they are finally overcome.

The spiritual world view accommodates the certainty that we all have invisible guides, so to speak, who are lovingly watching over our progress, and that we have a higher self, a spiritual principle, towards which we must perpetually aspire. All our sufferings are designed to teach us to overcome our lower desires, so that each of us may reunite with his or her own higher self.

2 | Spiritual Awakening in Our Time

"Oh, for the wonder that bubbles into my soul."
D.H. Lawrence

A SENSE OF WONDER is one of the factors that characterizes the awakening of the new age. It arises in part from the sense of the sacredness of all life working through all diversity. We are passing out of an epoch in which we were mere observers, distinct, isolated and alienated from an infinite number of disparate things. The experience of solitude was necessary — a prelude to the imaginative vision of the kinship with all life, and of the fact that mankind is in reality one great family. The poets and prose writers of the Romantic Movement recognized Imagination as that faculty which could apprehend the Whole, and by doing so restore to the soul what the analyzing intellect and sense-bound perception had taken from it. Keats wrote, "I am certain of nothing but the holiness of the heart's affection and the truth of Imagination." We must, however, ask in what sense imagination *is* true. The emerging world view helps us answer that question in much the same way that Coleridge, in "Religious Musings," did 175 years ago:

> There is one mind, one omnipresent mind
> Omnific. His most holy name is Love.
> Truth of subliming import! . . . . . .
>   'Tis the sublime in man
> Our noontide majesty, to know ourselves
> Parts and proportions of one wondrous whole!
> This fraternizes man, this constitutes

> *Our charities and bearings. But 'tis God*
> *Diffused through all, that doth make all one whole.*

It is precisely such understanding which is rising to consciousness again, both among older people and in a new generation of youth. We are beginning, perhaps dimly as yet, to *see* that behind and within the outer forms of matter is one life, manifesting in infinite variety and diversity. With an inner eye, we are looking into this whole, with what Coleridge called "sacred sympathy" — for once perceived as part of that whole, everything alive becomes sacred. Every form is a housing for Being. Each is therefore a window into the eternal worlds. Each is a navel for the universe of spirit, each a vortex leading our sight into the etheric planes. Creative Oneness has manifested itself through infinite diversity; but our consciousness now is emerging from its imprisonment in matter to find it can extend and unite itself with the organic oneness of things. As Wordsworth says:

> *To me the meanest flower that breathes can bring*
> *Thoughts that do often lie too deep for tears.*

A crystal, a bird, a single leaf can trigger this new understanding. Thus, meditation on a single object can lead one through to an empirical recognition that we as human beings are intimately and inextricably part of the whole of nature. In this way, we proceed to discover that Planet Earth is truly alive, a sentient creature with her own breathing, bloodstream, glands and consciousness. We human beings are integrally part of this organism, like blood corpuscles in a body. We are, moreover, points of consciousness for the Earth Being. Man is that point where, as Teilhard de Chardin says, "evolution becomes conscious of itself" and can think out into the cosmos. And having done that, we discover that the cosmos itself is shot through with living Thought, Intelligence and Creative Imagining. We can then begin to share what Wordsworth experienced in his famous musings at Tintern Abbey:

> . . . . . *I have felt*
> *A presence that disturbs me with the joy*
> *Of elevated thoughts: a sense sublime*
> *Of something far more deeply interfused*
> *Whose dwelling is the light of setting suns*
> *And the round ocean and the living air*
> *And the blue sky and in the mind of man,*
> *A motion and a spirit that impels*
> *All thinking things, all objects of all thoughts*
> *And rolls through all things.*

Raynor Johnson, in his book *Watcher on the Hill*, has collected many examples of "ordinary" people in our own time who have had a sudden flash — perhaps only a few seconds or minutes in duration — in which they have *seen* the life in nature and in man. All color in flowers and trees and sky is enhanced and intensified, color is even experienced as sound, everything appears extraordinarily beautiful and burgeoning with significance; and the seer knows with profound certainty that he has glimpsed the Reality behind appearance. All who have undergone this phenomenon concur that life will never be the same again, and that it will be invested with a quality of hope, of joy and of serene confidence unknown before. And such experiences are becoming ever more frequent. R.M. Bucke, in his book *Cosmic Consciousness*, describes a characteristic experience:

> *Like a flash there is presented to his consciousness a clear conception, a vision in outline of the meaning and drift of the universe. He does not come to believe merely, but he sees and knows that the cosmos, which to the self-conscious mind seems made up of dead matter, is in fact far otherwise, is in very truth a living*

presence. He sees that instead of men being, as it were, patches of life scattered through an infinite sea of non-living substance, they are in reality specks of relative death in an infinite ocean of life. He sees that the life which is in man is eternal, as all life is eternal, that the soul of man is as immortal as God is, that the universe is so built and ordered that without any peradventure all things work together for the good of each and all and that the foundation principle of the world is what we call 'Love' and that the happiness of every individual is, in the long run, absolutely certain. Especially does he obtain such a conception of the whole, or at least of an immense whole as dwarfs all conception, imagination or speculation, springing from and belonging to ordinary self-consciousness, such a conception as makes the old attempts mentally to grasp the universe and its meaning petty and ridiculous.

This note of joy is a real sign of the new age. It seems to run through so many of the contemporary groups that characterize our era. Despite often difficult and adverse contingencies, the soul can nevertheless be flooded with joy and confidence through the vision of its eternal nature and the certainty that it is on the path to the worlds of light and oneness.

Thus the whole of life becomes sacred. And once the same divinity is seen to be working within all diversity, all aspects of daily life begin to take on something of a ritual character. Meditation becomes a necessity at some time during the day, for during this period the stilled consciousness is lifted to approach the higher worlds. It is a ritual of inner listening which leads to a blending with the Creative Intelligence.

The spiritual world view, once experienced, cannot but permeate all our thoughts and actions. Attitudes then begin to change. Many people, for instance, both young and old, find they must change diet. It becomes essential to eat whole foods, organically grown. Many feel compelled to become vegetarian. Not only does flesh become distasteful, but it appears unthinkable to take animal life for the purpose of eating. Instead, one learns to live on the life forces within plant and fruit and grain. And the eating of fresh and uncooked food becomes both a delight and a necessity. Moreover, the need to give thanks to the beings which have produced such food becomes appropriate — a natural and sincere thing to do. The meal, then, like all else, becomes a new ritual. Partaking of the new pattern entails simplification. We must get closer to the heart of life, and too many things or too complex an existence are barriers to our exploration.

There are other dimensions to the spiritual world view as well. Even if one is in no sense clairvoyant, one awakens to the certainty of invisible planes of consciousness interweaving with our material world — regions peopled by those we love, who have moved on through the gate of physical death. One learns that they have telepathic contact with us and — since they are beyond space and time — can respond instantly to a call sent up to them with love and thanks. This offers further possibilities of inner communion — with both our minds and our hearts.

As we have stated, the inner being in each of us is immortal. It cannot be touched by the "death" which will break down the discarded sheath of the body. This recognition of the spiritual entity in man has immense implications. We are a creature of body, soul and *spirit* — and the spiritual being within us, the true "I," is imperishable. It always was and always will be.

In the first centuries of the Christian epoch this was accepted, as it had been in the ancient mysteries. But in 869 A.D., the 8th Ecumenical Council at Constantinople, under Pope Nicholas I, decreed that it would in future be heresy to speak of an immortal spiritual entity. Man was to be regarded as a duality, a creature of body and soul, and all spiritual qualities were categorized as mere adjuncts of the latter. Spirit, in short, was denied its divinity, was thrown back, so to speak, into the mundane world of limited reason and the senses. Thus sundered from its source, it assumed the forms by which we recognize it today — self-consciousness, intellectual pride and arrogance. And during the last two centuries, doctrines have proliferated that even attempt to show that soul is a fallacy, that man is a physical body and nothing more. Despite their pioneering work in fields of extrasensory perception, the most scientists will conclude from their remarkable discoveries is that the physical body has subtle and invisible vibrations and attributes. Soul is dismissed as nonexistent. The spiritual awakening in our time attempts to restore both soul and spirit to their proper status. It seeks to reestablish the realization that the essential nature of man is immortal spirit, and that the soul body and physical body are the sheaths necessary for life on the earth plane.

This position restores a meaning and coherence to life. Every event takes on intensified significance, and the world becomes an endless adventure, an immense opportunity for realization of the true individuality on ever finer spheres of being. We are now, one might say, reversing the edict of Pope Nicholas I and reinstating man as a spiritual being. The implications of this are enormous. But it is important to remember that we are not talking about a religious revival or a proselytizing movement. We are talking rather about a transformation in consciousness, such as occurred at the beginning of the Christian era, at the Renaissance and at the so-called Enlightenment — which, in many respects, was anything but that. We are talking about a new channelling of energies of Higher Intelligence, a recognition of guidance from the invisible and the possibility of widening consciousness to blend with the inner worlds of light. This entails, in one individual after another, a veritable transfiguration of mankind. And it brings in turn a "gentling" of human nature — particularly necessary in an age when so many lost souls, in apprehension and doubt, are succumbing to panic and violence.

A new age is being born and a new society is forming, composed of those who have found within themselves the power of light and love. The spiritual within man unites with the spiritual in the cosmos, and out of this union a new order begins to crystallize.

In this new order all living things are experienced as divine. A quite new orientation takes shape. Teilhard de Chardin called it "homing upon the Omega point." The soul, the human monad, experiences internally its goal and path of reuniting with the Divine Source from which it descended; and, like a homing pigeon, it sets its course to find the unity (or numinous) which is there to be born again within the heart. In our chaotic world this obviously offers an immense and forgotten prospect of home. And the big evolutionary picture *is* essential to us. Mankind has evolved to an unprecedented degree of ego-centered self-consciousness, with all its desolating sense of aloneness and separation. He has reached the point in his evolution where he may transcend that state, may discover that his inner being is spiritual, immortal and already one with the Whole. The barriers between the worlds are beginning to crumble. Inner and outer worlds are, as we are beginning to see, intimately and inextricably linked. Release of consciousness becomes possible, so that the soul may expand beyond its bodily limitations.

Toynbee, in his *Study of History*, contends that one sign of a declining civilization is the phenomenon of direct inner contact with the spiritual sources. It becomes possible for the individual to drink from the spiritual springs of being. On this basis, Toynbee compares our civilization to that of the Roman Empire in its decline. Then, in the catacombs, a new seed impulse began to blossom, which shook the world. In our time, a new ardor is stirring with a similar quality, a similar effluence of love and joy. Now, as then, a great impulse overlights mankind. Every death is also a rebirth. Every wintry decline is an occasion for the bursting of a new spring. This applies both to the life of an individual and to that of a culture. And again, free choice is always open to us. We can, if we wish, direct our attention solely to the symptoms of disintegration in our time — and very unpleasant, not to say alarming, some of them are. Alternatively, we can choose to watch the first bursting of the new spring; and the pace at which it is doing so is phenomenal. Over the broadest conceivable spectrum, spiritual knowledge is breaking through. The power of the living spirit, seeping through human consciousness like fresh water, bubbling up like fresh springs, blowing like a fine clean wind, is sweeping away the barriers between worlds. As Francis Thompson proclaims:

> *Oh world invisible we view thee,*
> *Oh world intangible we touch thee,*
> *Oh world unknowable we know thee,*
> *Inapprehensible, we clutch thee.*

And, to quote Teilhard:

> *We must put in the forefront of our concrete preoccupations the systematic arrangement and exploration of our universe, understood as the true home of mankind. Then material energy will circulate, and, more important still, spiritual energy will find its natural outlet in the attack launched against the mysteries of the World. The time has come to realize that Research is the highest human function, embracing the spirit of War and bright with the splendor of Religion. To keep up a constant pressure on the surface of the Real, is not that the supreme gesture of faith in Being, and therefore the highest form of adoration? All that is ours, if we understand how to avoid stifling within us the Spirit of Earth.*
>
> *Whoever wishes to be part of this spirit must die and be born again, for others and for himself. In order to reach this higher plane of humanity, he must bring about a complete transformation in his whole sense of values and his whole action.*

Nor is it only poets and mystics who are embracing a spiritual world view. Sir James Jeans, the great physicist, wrote:

> *The stream of human knowledge is impartially heading towards a non-mechanical reality: the universe begins to look more like a great thought than a great machine. Mind no longer appears to be an accidental intruder into the realm of matter. We are beginning to suspect that we ought rather to hail it as the creator and governor of this realm.*

And Einstein, another great scientific seer, states, "Religion without science is blind and science without religion is lame."

This great spiritual advance manifests itself, naturally, in a multitude of diverse ways. The object of the directing intelligence is clearly to sweep new shoals of souls into spiritual understanding. No one way of approach could achieve so vast a task. For some, the path will be one of deep and intensified thought, for some a surge of love, for some a training of the will, for some healing, for some a new awakening within the churches, for many a new development of the inner life that brings it into direct contact with the source. No one path is the only right one. We might almost say that the spiritual worlds show great wit and humor in throwing into the pool new dynamic ideas which will shake people out of their fixed positions and galvanize new interest. One's task is clearly to find one's own most appropriate personal path and to learn tolerance and discrimination in meeting all others who have found theirs. And what appear at first to be contradictions often prove to be polarities or paradoxes — the only verbal expression possible for the otherwise inexpressible. We are all striving to climb the same mountain. All ways lead to the summit, but not all ways suit everyone. Each must choose a way or be thrown into some confusion. And certain of the more direct routes are admittedly dangerous.

We are in the second Elizabethan Age, the second Renaissance. In the first, our ancestors explored the seas and discovered new continents, new tracts of the physical world. Those who failed to master the new arts of navigation risked drowning, but the goals of Drake and Raleigh were worth the risk. In our present Elizabethan Age, we are setting out to explore the cosmos and reality. True, our rockets may reach the moon and beyond, but the spiritual awakening of our time is an exploration of inner space. And of course it is dangerous. We are approaching fields in which the soul can well be lost if it allows itself to function recklessly or irresponsibly. Yet such dangers must not deter us from exploration. And nothing will stop the contemporary surge of investigation into esoteric wisdom, just as nothing will stop man from space exploration. We must recognize the dangers and learn to distinguish between valid and invalid paths of inquiry. And we may be certain that we have invisible guides and helpers who can lead us through to the light.

But there is also a sense of urgency. We are approaching a crucial turning point, and this generation is involved in a great task. Either man learns the true healing impulse of blending consciously with the powers of light, or he will plunge himself into disaster and catastrophe. Much may have to fall away in our present social structures, but a new society may then emerge in which the unifying spiritual impulse is genuinely at work. For there are springs of creative energy which can never run dry because they tap the eternal reservoirs of love and Creative imagining.

If changes are imminent, it is important that as many souls as possible awaken to their spiritual nature and be able to discern what is happening. In consequence, the immediate present is a time of profound growth and mind-opening—a resurgence of the spirit linking individuals and injecting fresh impulses into man's understanding. And as the pressure of inner and outer change increases, all who have touched their spiritual realities will comprehend what is occurring. We are truly involved with a Second Coming. Essentially, all is well, despite the ostensibly proliferating difficulties. But we need the courage to see that something tremendous is upon us — the majesty of a New Birth on a planetary and a cosmic scale — and that we are all a part of it. The only *real* anxiety is that we may not be awake and aware when our moment comes.

3 | The Ageless Wisdom Reemerges

W E HAVE SPOKEN of new knowledge. It *is* new and fresh, yet it is also as old as civilization. It is indeed the ageless wisdom, the wisdom of the ancients reappearing in a form appropriate to our intellectual age. This, the stream of esoteric or secret wisdom, has flowed like a clear underground current through every epoch of history, emerging in varying forms to influence minds in each generation able to receive its nourishment. It is the knowledge descended from exalted spiritual teachers. It was set down by the Holy Rishis in the Upanishads of ancient India. It is the secret meaning behind the sacred books of ancient Persia. In the temples of Chaldea, Egypt and Greece, the ageless wisdom was transmitted to candidates for initiation in the mystery schools. These selected individuals, worthy of the knowledge about to be conferred upon them, were subjected to rigorous training, disciplines and ordeals, culminating frequently in the ritual known as the "Temple Sleep." Manly P. Hall, describing the initiation by the priests in the Great Pyramid, writes:

The candidate was laid in the great stone coffin and for three days his spirit, freed from its mortal coil, wandered at the gateways of eternity: His KA, as a bird, flew through the spiritual spheres of space. He discovered that all the universe was life, progress and eternal growth. Realizing that his body was a house which he could slip out of and return to without death, he achieved actual im-

*mortality. At the end of three days, he returned to himself again,
and having thus personally and actually experienced the great
mystery, he was indeed an Initiate — one who beheld and one to
whom religion had fulfilled her duty, bringing him to the Light of
God.*

Such methods of initiation are, needless to say, wholly un-
suitable for modern man, yet the same essential truth demands
attainment in other ways.

Over the Temple of Delphi was carved the inscription: "Man,
know thyself and thou shalt know the Universe." This relation
of man to the living cosmos is entirely lost in our materialistic
culture. The initiate priests knew that man was a microcosm
reflecting and embodying the macrocosm. "Who has put wisdom
in the inward parts?" In the human organism is the wisdom
of the cosmos, and man as archetypal idea was first in the
creation, though last to appear in physical evolution.

Such teachings are essentially aspects of the spiritual world
view. They revealed the divine origin of the human spirit, its
imperishable quality, its descent into the limitations of the
body upon earth, the meaning of its trials and the reality of
the higher worlds to which it would return. And he who di-
vulged the secrets of the Mysteries was punished by death. The
chief reason for this was that the ordinary man was simply not
equipped to handle revelations which were too puissant for his
limited consciousness and soul.

In ancient times, the wisdom in question was made accessible to the public at large in symbolic form, through myth,
legend and drama. These served as conducting mediums, so to
speak, and also as insulation — much as modern electronic apparatus concentrates, channels and protects us from a force
that, in its raw form, might prove destructive. But myth, allegory and legend were certainly no simplistic inventions of
simple or primitive folk. On the contrary, they are repositories
for a profound and potent wisdom. The collective unconscious

of a race, or the genius of an individual, uses such vehicles as a channel by means of which the higher worlds can give to man the great truths about the nature of the soul in a form it can accept, and which will strengthen it in its growth. Hence their immense significance, as recognized by C.G. Jung.

All over the world, myths and fairy stories tell in their thousand variants the same great tale of the soul's descent from higher worlds into the limitations of matter. They impart to the young mind a spiritual picture of life. Paradoxically, therefore, one of the great bulwarks against such materialistic doctrines as Marxism would be the telling of fairy stories to the child, thereby building into the young soul, if only subconsciously, the certainty of its divine origin and spiritual destiny. In our intellectual age, the reinterpreting of the myths is a great and important channel for knowledge. The soul knows the truth which, when assimilated and interpreted by the mind, causes the heart to leap with joy to embrace it.

The Mysteries continued into the Roman epoch in a debased form. Then the Empire, under Constantine, was converted to Christianity. When all Roman citizens were compelled to take the faith and a great priesthood had to deal with large numbers, the secret teachings were inevitably driven further underground and subjected to persecution. Christ Himself had sent the gifts of the spirit and insisted that the individual could make direct contact with spiritual worlds. His disciples received, developed and practiced what He had taught them, but the later priesthood declared such practices heretical. Through subsequent centuries, they were suppressed as witchcraft and heresy. In consequence, the great esoteric teachings were passed on to Gnostic sects, like the Cathars, or through secret teachings or orders like the Knights Templar, the Rosicrucians and the Masons. Many of these, too — the Templars, for example — were suppressed and cruelly persecuted. Many naturally became debased and lost their original intention, their original purity. But the ageless wisdom, lighting up in esoteric Christianity, runs like a golden thread through Western history, appearing in a guise appropriate for each successive age. We are now experiencing a new manifestation of it, uniquely suited to our own epoch. This is the rising tide of which we have spoken, which offers a new hope and certainty for mankind.

A great turning point occurred at the end of the 19th Century. By that time, Western man had reached a period known to esoteric wisdom as the end of the Kali Juga, or Dark Age — an era, that is, in which the possibility of the individual opening his consciousness to spiritual worlds had become increasingly difficult. Religious forms might continue, but only as empty forms, while direct knowledge of higher worlds had become virtually impossible. Immediately afterwards, however, this bleak situation reversed itself — a fact to which the ever-mounting interest in spiritual knowledge bears witness. And this time, the ageless wisdom was disseminated by seers in terms that suited the highly developed intellectuality of the period. Blavatsky's *Secret Doctrine*, Annie Besant's Theosophy, Steiner's Anthroposophy and Alice Bailey's esoteric writings all herald a resurgence of spiritual energy issuing from both east and west. A veritable flood of books and papers on esoteric subjects was soon being published — and continues to be so today. It exerted a profound influence on the great cultural figures of the time, as well as on pioneers in psychology like C.G. Jung. Now, the secret wisdom is accessible to all who are able to receive it. Moreover, it has become accessible not only to groups, but to individuals, provided they adhere to the right paths. Attaining it is a quest of immeasurable importance, fraught, of course, with dangers, but offering immense recompense and reward. For many people today, it has become the true purpose of life on earth. It may ultimately prove the key to the redemption of mankind.

It is now clearer than ever that the human body is itself the temple into which the spirit descends. Greek temples offered the God a chamber in which it might touch down upon earth.

In a very profound sense, we now need no temple, for the body offers the chamber which can allow divinity to come to birth in each individual heart. Thus, every man is responsible for his own body as the temple for the new mysteries; he must prepare it by cleansing the blood through appropriate diet, correct breathing, training and meditation. The body must become an organ through which the light and fire of the spirit can work to overcome the darkness of our environment. Our polluted world can be redeemed only if man so transforms himself that the very cells of his body bear and carry the radiant light of the spirit. This point is wonderfully demonstrated in Mary Fullerson's book, *The Form of the Fourth*.

In light of this, we can begin to recognize how much the temples of man reflect the human body. It is as if the great architects externalized in their buildings their own experience of themselves. Sometimes this may have been unconscious, but research into lost knowledge confirms that immense wisdom was often deliberately built into temples and cathedrals. The proportions of the body are as the harmonies of music, and are reflected again in the great edifices of worship. There is also reason to believe that the so-called subtle bodies of man, with their etheric centers or chakras, are also represented in churches and cathedrals. If man is indeed the microcosm reflecting and embodying the macrocosm, then within the miracle of the body must be enshrined all the secrets of the cosmos.

4 | School of Earth

THE GENERAL POSTULATE we must consider and at least entertain (not necessarily believe or accept) is that the universe is shot through with living intelligence, that matter is derivative from creative spirit, that the true nature of man is a droplet of the divine source and that the human mind can experience itself in lifted consciousness as part of a stupendous whole.

If we posit the spirit as an eternal being, we must necessarily conclude that it existed before we were born as individuals. It descends into incarnation, in other words, as an already developed entity. The implications of this premise are immense. Firstly, it offers a very different perspective to those of materialistic culture on the question of survival after death. At a single leap, we can perceive that life is inextinguishable, that the drop of divinity cannot be eradicated. If the kernel of man is eternal and imperishable, survival becomes axiomatic— simply because there can be no death in the sense of the extinction of man's integral, quintessential being. One asks whether one believes in the all-encompassing Oneness only when one has already lost it; if one knows it, the question does not even arise, simply because it is not a matter of belief, but of the certainty that accompanies direct knowledge. In the same way, uncertainty of survival after physical death will be rendered irrelevant if we recognize that the spirit is an eternal drop of divinity.

A much more important problem is preexistence. Whereas desire for survival derives from personal preoccupations, preexistence introduces much graver issues of responsibility and purpose. When a child asks "where it came from," it is really asking, "What is the memory I have of a wonderful world of light?" It is not, despite the assumptions of our materialistic culture, asking for premature information about sexuality and the so-called "facts of life." Memory of a world of wonder may well survive through childhood, for, as we have said, the descent into a body at birth is a descent into drastic limitation and constriction. To contemplate this diminution is staggering. An immortal soul, heir to all the breadth of untrammelled consciousness — a free spirit able to range serenely through the wide realms of spirit, to rise towards the spiritual sun, to move blithely in the "country of the summer stars" — an entity of such majestic proportions must now undertake to enclose and confine itself within a puny physical frame. When we contemplate a newborn child, it is inappropriate to say, "Look at this tiny soul." What we are contemplating is, on the contrary, a mature and perhaps great soul entering and occupying a tiny body. We falsify the truth if we identify the majestic developed soul with the puling, crying little body. Here, developing before our eyes, is the miracle of the formation in matter of a vehicle which can carry an eternal spiritual being. A Leonardo, a Saint Francis, a Napoleon is a colossal being, a peak of humanity; but each has to submit to limitation within a bodily frame. There is equality in the physical, but not on the soul and spiritual level. We are not our bodies. Rather, we live through our bodies and discard them when their usefulness ceases.

We must learn to see birth as, in a true sense, a descent into the tomb of a body, and death as the release again into light and expansion of awareness. The earth plane is obviously full of difficulties, and its pressures on the free spirit are enormous. The senses, as we have seen, are but filters. We must recognize these restrictions, through which the soul must pass once it enters the narrow gate of birth. From freedom to move at the speed of thought, it is confined to the painfully slow pace of bodily progress. We could, after all, hardly carry on our daily concerns at the flashing speed of free spirits like Ariel. And if we contemplate the stupendous process occurring in the growth of a baby, we will not be surprised that there are troubles in growing up — particularly when the eternal soul has failed to find a body really suitable to its needs. This may be a clue to many of the maladjusted or mentally handicapped children of our time. They need not be weak-minded or backward. They might, on the contrary, be highly advanced souls who have failed to find a suitable body, and therefore the spirit cannot truly incarnate, cannot accommodate itself comfortably to its physical frame and nervous system.

Poets so often express for us these profound truths. Thomas Traherne, for example, writing in the early 17th Century, describes his faculty for remembering his life not only in the womb, but even before. It is perhaps no mere coincidence that Traherne's works were lost and only rediscovered in the late 19th Century, an age which could at last begin to understand and appreciate them. For — if we accept what he offers us — we have in some of Traherne's work a firsthand account of preexistence. In the poem "The Praeparative," there is a verse, obviously referring to the embryo, which ends:

> *I was within,*
> *A house I knew not; newly cloath'd with Skin.*
> *Then was my Soul my only All to me,*
> *A living endless Ey,*
> *Scarce bounded with the Sky,*
> *Whose Power, and Act, and Essence was to see;*
> *I was an inward Sphere of Light,*
> *Or an interminable Orb of Sight,*
> *Exceeding that which makes the Days,*

A vital Sun that shed abroad its Rays:
All Life, all Sense,
A naked, simple, pure Intelligence.

Such, if we can accept Traherne's testimony, is the experience of the free soul before entering bodily limitation. It provides much food for thought for parents and teachers, and intensifies our sense of wonder.

In the same connection, it is worth reconsidering Wordsworth's well-known "Ode on the Intimations of Immortality in early Childhood":

Our birth is but a sleep and a forgetting:
The soul that rises with us, our life's star,
Hath had elsewhere its setting,
And cometh from afar;
Not in entire forgetfulness,
And not in utter nakedness,
But trailing clouds of glory do we come
From God, who is our home.
Heaven lies about us in our infancy;
Shades of the prison-house begin to close
Upon the growing boy,
But he beholds the light, and whence it flows,
He sees it in his joy;
The youth, who daily farther from the east
Must travel, still is Nature's priest,
And by the vision splendid
Is on his way attended;
At length the man perceives it die away,
And fade into the light of common day.

The dying of the vision, however, is not the final end. It is followed by a rebirth in our later years. Our task now is to revive "the vision splendid" and to grasp with the knowledge of the heart the tremendous implications of Wordsworth's intuition and Traherne's memory.

This task of our later years can alter our attitude to old age. We have seen that we are not justified in speaking of the newborn child as a "tiny soul." The soul is immortal and therefore does not age. And for that very reason, we should not speak of an aging person as a "poor old soul." The earthly sheath may begin to break down as years advance, but the spiritual being which inhabits it and uses it should then be freeing itself from the fetters of body and personality. The later years of life should be an experience of mounting anticipation before what the future holds. Once we recognize that so-called death is but a release from limitation, and that the eternal being has possibilities of endless exploration and advance, we will understand how vitally important the later years of life are. It is lamentable that so many approach the Great Transition with so little preparation for it. They are like students entering a university of the spirit without even troubling to take one "O" Level examination. And such inadequate preparation makes a difference, for the spirit carries with it into the beyond only that which it has been able to spiritualize through its faculties and its creativity on earth.

It is a marvelous dispensation of fate that in our era, medical advances have given us a dozen free years, more or less, to harvest the experience of a lifetime and prepare for the future. This has never before occurred on so large a scale in the entire course of human history. Until recently, life, save for the fortunate few, has consisted of nurture followed by toil to the point of utter exhaustion. But now, our whole attitude towards retirement and old age can change as we awaken to the unreality of death and the supreme hope proffered by the eternal quality of life. We can now come to realize that it is infinitely worthwhile for the future of the soul to develop spiritual understanding and keep alive the creative faculties in preparation for passing on to the planes of wider awareness after the body has been abandoned. In consequence, our attitudes towards the process of aging will greatly change. We will begin to see the establishment of clinics or nursing homes dedicated to the joyful passage into the beyond.* Instead of hushing up death as if it were something not quite "nice" to mention, we will face it in all its grandeur, and people will learn to accept the release it offers with anticipation, relief and joy. As W.B. Yeats writes in one of his most famous poems, "Sailing to Byzantium":

> An aged man is but a paltry thing,
> A tattered coat upon a stick, unless
> Soul clap its hands and sing, and louder sing
> For every tatter in its mortal dress.
> Nor is there singing school but studying
> Monuments of its own magnificence;
> And therefore I have sailed the seas and come
> To the holy city of Byzantium.

This verse offers the true key to adult education in later years. To Yeats, Byzantium represents a higher level of consciousness, a totally different dimension of being and reality, as well as a wonderful symbolic city. We may perhaps say that the singing school of the soul is not only study of its past achievements, but also the living ideas from the eternal plane which break into our consciousness with illumination, inspiring us with a vision of the worlds of spirit. As T.S. Eliot writes:

> Old men ought to be explorers
> Here and there does not matter
> We must be still and still moving

* Written in 1977, this thought anticipates the development of the Hospice Movement and the work of Dr. Elizabeth Kübler-Ross.

Into another intensity
For a further union, a deeper communion . . .
In my end is my beginning.

If we accept the working hypothesis that the kernel of man
is a droplet of divinity, and therefore immortal, we will obtain
a more profound understanding of Blake's dictum:

We are put on earth a little space
That we may learn to bear the beams of love.

This again implies purposeful descent for the sake of an educational experience. Only in the field of gravity can we learn
certain lessons, and the trials we undergo are a strengthening
of the soul to enable it to "bear the beams of love."

We might well ask why the descent into matter should be
so necessary. The answer is that each soul must pass through
the initiatory experience of separation, isolation and aloneness.
We must undergo the agony of being — at least apparently —
cut off from the divine, an agony that can only be experienced
in the gravity field of earth. Man is a spiritual being who has
been given the divine gift of free will. For this reason, he has
been called the 10th Hierarchy.

What is man that Thou art mindful of him
Or the son of man that Thou visitest him?
For Thou hast made him a little lower than the angels
And crowned him with glory and honor.

Possessing this God-like attribute, man has the opportunity of
developing as a free moral being, so that he may return to the
divine of his own free choice. Thus man has been called "the
experiment of God." The world of matter, ruled by gravity, is
the setting necessary for this experience of separation and exercise of free will. Only by separation from the divine and from

the realms of light can man discover his freedom. And his spiritual guides must undoubtedly watch with some anxiety what man does with his self-consciousness and the freedom that attends it. He must prove himself worthy of the gift conferred upon him.

The divine purpose seems to be that man should have the opportunity of growing into a companion and co-creator with God. To date, however, he has tragically abused the trust reposed in him. Isabella, in Shakespeare's *Measure for Measure*, describes our failure thus:

> . . . . . *Proud man*
> *Set in a little brief authority,*
> *Most ignorant of what he's most assured,*
> *His glassy essence, like an angry ape*
> *Plays such fantastic tricks before high heaven*
> *As make the angels weep.*

The "glassy essence" is of course the light-filled higher self belonging to the eternal worlds of spirit. Of this, man is "most assured"; it is not a figment of his imagination. But man must pass through the long and arduous phase of self-consciousness, taking his full measure of power, satisfaction of desire, aggression and egoism, suffering and loss, before he discovers that his true and eternal task is to reunite with his higher self and work for the development of his eternal spiritual individuality, which can expand into consciousness of the cosmos and of God.

Each of us, therefore, must accept the inevitable ordeal of loneliness and its attendant suffering:

> *Alone, alone, all all alone*
> *Alone on a wide, wide sea,*
> *And never a saint took pity on*
> *My soul in agony.*

Thus laments the Ancient Mariner in Coleridge's profound allegory. We are each of us that mariner, voyaging through life, having committed some sin symbolized by the shooting of the albatross. With the curse around our neck, our "ship" held up in the doldrums, we incur the nightmare of life-in-death. But when, from the heart and through our own initiative, we turn towards the true beauty and unity of life surrounding us, the curse is dispelled, a fresh wind blows, the ship speeds towards "home," and the mariner, passing through a blessed "sleep of death," is released into a higher state of consciousness.

If the earth plane is indeed the great training ground of the soul, it is unlikely that we should come here only once. One life is hardly sufficient to reap all the harvest of experience that earth can offer. If the nature of the soul is eternal, moreover, its being so entails that we were already alive as developed entities before we were born. And from this it follows that we must choose voluntarily to descend into the earth vibration when there is a soul-lesson to be learnt. Furthermore, the consciousness of the very Earth-Being itself is evolving, and, within it, the racial consciousness of mankind. It is illogical to embrace the theory of evolution while denying that man's consciousness and spiritual being evolve similarly from age to age. In every epoch, there are vital lessons which can only be learnt by taking the plunge and reentering bodily existence with its accompanying experience of separation. History, to hark back to our previous analogy, may be likened to a great school. We must move from class to class, allowing each to offer its unique lesson. No one would presume to believe that by entering the 4th form for one term we are qualified to sit for a diploma.

This concept of the School of Earth was developed first by the German philosopher Gotthold Ephraim Lessing in a treatise on "The Education of the Human Race" written in 1780. Lessing's essay was one of the first coherent exoteric expressions of the doctrine of reincarnation to appear in modern Western culture. He concludes his work with the splendid query, "Is not the whole of eternity mine?" If we ask ourselves the same question, adult education may truly become an endless adventure!

That we return to earth repeatedly has always been accepted as axiomatic in the East. There, however, the concept has been linked with the "wheel of rebirth," a return into incarnation again and again until desire has at last been transcended. Buddhism, for example, sees suffering as the specific product of desire, and freedom from suffering is achieved when desires cease. Then the soul is released to move on to Nirvana.

Since its widespread appearance in western culture and consciousness at the beginning of this century, the idea of reincarnation has itself evolved. While many now find the general principle acceptable, opinion differs about a number of more specific details. Given the western preoccupation with individuality, for example, there is often a rather superficial desire simply to find out "who one was" in a previous life. Such crude oversimplifications of an immensely complicated issue should be avoided. Any form of guesswork or speculation is unjustified and even dangerous, for it can only lead to self-deception, frequently based on arrogance and wishful thinking. The subject must be approached only with great reticence and discretion. Rudolf Steiner, in his early investigations, showed what advanced spiritual knowledge and technique were required for conscious research in the field. Edgar Cayce, the American sensitive, showed how many of our illnesses arise from happenings in earlier lives and how often cures can be achieved if the true source is disclosed. Granted, then, that conscious communion with teachers in the "beyond" can sometimes offer useful indications as to earlier lives. But one can only conlude that — while it is valuable to grasp the general principles of reincarnation — little is to be gained by mere spurious curiosity. The requisite knowledge will be forthcoming from the higher worlds as and when it will prove necessary and helpful.

Nevertheless, because the West has always been more absorbed with individuality than the East, it is fitting for our western minds that evolutionary thinking should color our understanding of reincarnation. Consciousness evolves from age to age, and this consciousness is carried in individual souls. Each, therefore, can enter the stream of earth life as a creative deed to lift the race as a whole one step further. We descend not merely to undergo experiences for the benefit of our own souls, but to throw ourselves creatively into the great task of human development. Thus, the eastern "wheel of rebirth" is, in the West, transformed into a spiral staircase leading ultimately to "a new Heaven and a new earth." There is a certain nobility about this conception. For those not drawn to the spiritual world view, there is, of course, no obligation to accept the postulate of repeated earth lives. For many, however, that postulate brings illumination and accounts for the gross differences in individual misfortune or opportunity. The breadth of vision it implies lifts us above cruder materialism, bringing into our thinking a broader pattern of spiritual evolution. The eternal entity of man — existing from the beginning as an archetypal idea in the mind of God — begins at a certain stage to embody itself in the evolving physical body. Thus we arrive at two distinct yet concurrent streams of evolution. One produces a body ever approaching the ideal pattern of the original archetype. The other governs the spiritual development of the individual spirit, which dips for experience into a body, is released by death into wider consciousness, then plunges again into another sojourn on earth. In this way, the human spirit, while perfecting itself, simultaneously takes a creative part in the evolution of the body, which is the temple of earthly life.

An integral part of the picture of reincarnation is Karma, the Law of Compensation. "As ye sow, so shall ye reap." This is not to be understood as a blind working out of "an eye for an eye, a tooth for a tooth." Its true corollary is the principle, "Do unto others as you would have them do unto you," which, in very similar words, has been promulgated as the basic law for life by all founders and prophets of all the great religions. If man could adhere to this dictum, world harmony could indeed be achieved.

Everything we do, whatever its moral value, brings its compensation, either in this life or a subsequent one. Perhaps we can understand the principle more effectively in psychological terms. A certain weakness or predisposition in our character, for instance, draws us into situations and contacts which amount to temptations. If we "fall," the flaw responsible is strengthened and the same pattern will repeat itself until at last we become conscious of it and can overcome it. "To him that overcometh will be given the crown." And if, in one life, the necessary step has not been taken, it must be confronted again in the next. The principle is supremely logical. We bring trials and ordeals upon ourselves, and they can assume an infinite number of forms. If we indulge in self-pity, if we merely moan and complain about our misfortunes, if we wonder vindictively why "this should happen to us," it means we have not yet awakened to the significance of the law of compensation. Once we understand this law, on the other hand, we can adopt the courageous view that we are total cause of all we are and all that happens to us. Then we can discern our troubles and suffering as a species of soul training. They come to have for us a purgatorial quality, which, if correctly accepted, will enable us to take a further step in our inner development. What we are talking about, then, is an immense educational process designed to lift mankind from a low level of awareness into full self-awareness and self-knowledge. In every lifetime, we have the opportunity to lift ourselves further from the morass of sensual experience into clearer and purer consciousness. And we must remember that our destinies are presided over by intelligences far more advanced than ourselves. Study of the way the law of compensation works suggests a pattern of great subtlety and justice. It is said that "destiny is always kind."

The setback that afflicts us, though it may appear meaningless misfortune, must be treated as part of this developing pattern. Thus perceived, it provides us with the strength to endure it, and grow with it.

If we have badly wronged another in one life, it may be necessary to expiate the deed by returning to earth and meeting the same person in a later life, where we might, for example, make some great sacrifice on his behalf. Until this is accomplished, our own soul is held back in its upward journey towards the light. And ultimately, the advanced soul, having wholly transcended self and egoism, will be filled with a compassion and love for all being. At that point, it will no longer need to return to earthly incarnation for further training. If it does so, that will be only for the sake of pure service to the race.

Love, in short, is the solvent of Karma, which, we must remember, is not an inexorable law of punishment. Rather, it is a loving influence working on the souls of men until they can awaken to the spirit. Then there will truly be "joy in heaven" at the triumph of a soul which has genuinely "come through."

To grasp something of the working of the principle of reincarnation and Karma is essential if we are to understand history. This principle opens a vista that illumines both the life of the individual and that of the folk-soul — for we are all linked to our national or cultural Karma.

To summarize what we have said, the eternal essence of the human being makes a descent into a series of earthbound lives, thus building up a personality with which to confront the pressures of the world. The whole "object of the exercise" is, through long experience and suffering, to master and dissolve this lower self and transmute the soul into an organ in which the Higher Self, the true spiritual being of man, can operate. The ordinary personality is obviously too ephemeral to reincarnate. But at death we carry forward a seed of real individuality which, developing in the life between death and rebirth, can, when time is ripe, make the descent again.

If we could develop the capacity to remember down the corridors of time, we might recall the earlier ages of mankind as our own personal experience. In consequence, the principle of reincarnation and Karma profoundly enhances both the interest and relevance of history. In a significant sense, we *are* history, since the core of our being has been present in earlier epochs. And as greater understanding of the subject is acquired, we may expect important light to be thrown on many fields of research.

There is reason to believe, moreover, that souls incarnate in groups. Therefore, it is highly likely that those to whom we are drawn as friends, close colleagues, partners in love or marriage, or parent or child, are souls with whom we were together in previous lives. This concept, if accepted, greatly enhances our respect for our own group of close contacts and helps us to face the difficulties of personality inherent in the trials of earth life.

Preexistence implies that a soul chooses voluntarily to incarnate. At the same time, the spiritual guides and the Higher Self help us in the period before birth to find the right access into earth life. And this would entail, among other things, choosing our parents. Though such an idea might appear ridiculous at first, maturer consideration reveals it as a possibility which adds to the majesty of human life and the respect in which we hold the other fragments of divinity with whom we jointly participate in the earth struggle.

At this point, it would not be out of place to quote some verses from a poem by Robert Frost, "Trial by Existence":

> *Even the bravest that are slain*
> *Shall not dissemble their surprise*
> *On waking to find valor reign,*

Even as on earth, in paradise; . . .

And from a cliff-top is proclaimed
The gathering of the souls for birth,
The trial by existence named,
The obscuration upon earth . . .

And none are taken but who will,
Having first heard the life read out
That opens earthward, good and ill,
Beyond the shadow of a doubt . . .

Nor is there wanting in the press
Some spirit to stand simply forth,
Heroic in its nakedness,
Against the uttermost of earth . . .

But always God speaks at the end:
'One thought in agony of strife
The bravest would have by for friend,
The memory that he chose the life;
But the pure fate to which you go
Admits no memory of choice.
Or the woe were not earthly woe
To which you give the assenting voice . . .'

'Tis of the essence of life here,
Though we chose greatly, still to lack
The lasting memory at all clear,
That life has for us on the rack
Nothing but what we somehow choose;
Thus are we wholly stripped of pride
In the pain that has but one close,
Bearing it crushed and mystified.

5 | Death— The Great Adventure

Of all subjects requiring re-appraisal in light of the spiritual world view, death takes a paramount place. Ours is a death-ridden culture. Death, in one form or another, seems always to be the chief news. At the same time, it is a theme we try zealously to avoid. It is something not quite "nice" to talk about. It must be mentioned only in muted whispers, if at all. Every possible medical means must be employed to keep a person alive, even at immense cost in money, suffering and energy. In a great many minds, dread of death looms immensely large, a gigantic brooding specter. For others, there is a basic unconcern, a wilfully assumed indifference. As we can know so little about what, if anything, happens hereafter, it is best to ignore the whole unpleasant subject — this is the prevalent attitude.

Conditioned by the materialism of our time, we tend to identify ourselves with our bodies. In consequence, we wonder how consciousness can continue without the physical organ of the brain. This is perhaps the strongest argument of those who do not believe in survival after physical death. But even among believers and religious-minded people, the emphasis is constantly on *rest* in the hereafter: "Thou in the grave shalt rest . . ." "Rest in Peace" is the theme of inscriptions on thousands of tombstones. Some are deliberately witty, such as one in a church porch for a pauper:

The further in the more you pay
So here lie I as warm as they.

Or in the ballad "Clark Saunders":

My bed it is full lowly now,
Amang the hungry worms I sleep . . .
Cauld mould is my covering now
But and my winding sheet,
The dew it falls nae sooner down
Than my resting place is weet.

Quite obviously, such inscriptions incorporate the tacit assumption that we are identical with our bodies, or that the soul is tied to the body when the latter dies. But to those who believe in extinction of consciousness after death, and who demand proof of survival, perhaps the best reponse is a species of counterattack: "Can *you* produce for *me* one shred of real evidence that you are extinguished? I challenge you to demonstrate that your position is anything but sheer supposition. An immense body of circumstantial evidence is now available for any mind prepared to consider it openly, without prejudice. This evidence provides increasingly more basis to conclude that the soul continues, very much alive. There is no similar evidence to bear witness to its extinction."

It must be reemphasized that man in his core is an eternal being of spirit, housed for a time in a body. This truth about his manifold nature has largely been forgotten, and is only now being recovered. Furthermore, as a spiritual being, man belongs to the spiritual realms. In descending to earth life, he takes on drastic limitation and his five senses are really filters. They allow only fragments of the glory of creation's light and harmony to enter his consciousness. To think that this free spiritual being is identified with the discarded and rotting corpse, that it sleeps in the grave or is consumed in the fire of the crematorium, is sheer blindness arising from a circumscribed view. Our thought and imagination must appreciate that the free-ranging spiritual being can indeed venture further into the realms of light.

It is rather remarkable that there is no word in our language to imply or describe that most majestic and solemn of processes, the release of the soul into light. For this is what the passage through the gate of death truly entails. During the past few centuries, death has become almost exclusively associated with the hideous corpse and rotting cadaver. Dürer's "Dance of Death," for example, portrays the sinister form coming to tap us on the shoulder with its fearful summons. Now, however, it is time we broke definitively with this outdated attitude and recognized that the spiritual entity of man is imperishable. We should therefore drop from our vocabulary those words which identify the soul of man with the mechanical process by which the physical sheath decays and is discarded. We must awaken to the great realization that on all levels there can be no death without rebirth — in other words, without release onto a subtler and more light-filled plane of life. We may thus enjoy the certainty that the liberated soul is free to range in wide realms of existence and that vistas of exploration, joyous adventure and creative activity open up to us in the hereafter.

Everywhere in living nature, the process of death occurs solely in order that old forms may give way to new ones by a process of metamorphosis. Every death is accompanied by a resurrection, a new "becoming." As Goethe writes: "Nature invented death that there might be new life." The eternal being is released in order that it may assume a new form. The daffodil "dies" and is thrown onto the compost heap, where it breaks down into humus, the matrix of life. In the meantime, the seed holds the core of new living forms. In the soul of man, similarly, psychological death — the temporary death of the transient individual personality — is often necessary for an inner step to be taken. In a jocular mood, for example, William Blake wrote his own epitaph: "William Blake, who delighted in good company, born 1759 and died many times since." And Goethe again reiterates the profound truth:

For if you have not got this, this DEATH AND BECOMING,
You are but a dull guest in the dark world.

It is worth reexamining the subject of death from the hypothesis that the spiritual individuality of man (or what is loosely called the "soul") is imperishable. Released from the body, it is still itself, but moving now with greater freedom in a subtler world. Certainly this would seem to be confirmed by all communications received from the "beyond."

For the newly dead, it is often a surprise to find oneself very much alive and free from illness, aches and pains. It appears that our friends are there to meet us in surroundings at first much like the world to which we are accustomed, though more beautiful. The explanation is simple enough. The next world is composed from thought and imagination. It is a subtler plane of finer vibrations, and therefore substance is immediately responsive to mentation and intention. Thus, there are houses, trees and rivers which are experienced as solid since they are on the same vibratory rate as our new "bodies." We know that solid matter on earth feels hard to us but is in reality composed of widely spaced particles of energy. In a similar way, on higher and subtler planes, worlds created by imagining exist. There is a region of extraordinary beauty known as the "Summerland," which is described by many communicants. This is a soul place where the heart's desires are fulfilled. Having reached it, many feel it to be heaven and are content to sojourn there for substantial periods of time.

Of course it is true that this is a plane of illusion; but that does not make the experience of it any less real, valid or important. It is, after all, no more illusory than our own earth plane. The "Maya" of the material world is real and necessary enough for us while we are here. The crucial point to realize is that the genuine realms of spirit exist on far higher planes, attained only after long soul development and catharsis.

Before reaching the "Summerland," the departing soul passes through the "Borderland." After an initial period of sleep or unconsciousness, it wakes to find itself in surroundings formed really by its own preoccupations and preconceptions. The soul before death sends out "the call," and those it loves gather to receive it into the next world. Clearly this can be a supremely joyful moment, and those who have prepared their understanding may find they move quickly through to the plane of light.

What, however, of the many souls in our materialistic age who lack all certainty of the true reality of life after death? Many now are agnostic and even atheistic, and are thoroughly skeptical of survival. They, too, naturally, will awaken to find themselves alive. Many, in fact, will at first refuse to believe they have died. But if they are totally unprepared, they may find themselves in a fog or maze, or lost in some gloomy setting which is really the symbolic counterpart, the objectification, of their belief, or lack of it.

The important fact, confirmed by so many reports, is that friends and loved ones from the realm of light have difficulty establishing contact with a soul held in the thralls of blindness to the spirit. Until the soul is ready to respond, it cannot be reached from above. In the present age of disbelief, therefore, the "Borderland" is apparently a very dark place. Thousands of souls pass over without the comprehension that would enable them to make contact and break through. In consequence, there is a need for "rescue centers," where wanderers between death and new life can be awakened and redeemed.

We here on earth have an urgent role to play in the process. The soul after death will invariably turn back for contact with those it has loved. It can absorb knowledge from those still alive on earth. Indeed, the initial nourishment for the soul is drawn from the spiritual thoughts of those with whom it has affinities on earth, particularly when they are asleep. Today, however, when so many enter sleep at night without having developed any spiritual awareness, the crying need of the lost souls hungry for sustenance remains unanswered. Furthermore, when a person bereft on earth is filled with unreasoning grief, a species of smoke screen is created which prevents the soul in the beyond even finding its friend, much less establishing contact. Herein lies the immeasurable importance of reevaluating our conceptions of death. For souls moving on, it is essentially a release which can be filled with joy. The substance of so many communications is that "I am all right and very much alive and it is wonderful over here."

As for the sorrow of those of us left behind, we must be honest and acknowledge that it is sorrow largely for ourselves — a form of self-pity. Obviously we cannot belittle the pain of parting and the accompanying sense of loss. But we must accept the basic fact of telepathic contact. The higher world is a thought world. Those residing in it are free to move with immense rapidity, and souls can blend with each other, sharing consciousness. As a result, our thoughts, prayers and love for a departed friend are instantly received. Even though most of us cannot register this, we can nevertheless act on it. We should talk to our friends or relatives, bring them actively into our lives and plans, mentally discuss things with them. And we should support them with love and joy and courage as they explore ahead. Such an attitude preserves and validates our bond with the dead, but does not shackle them to earth in the wrong way. On the contrary, it is rather our unreasoning and persisting grief that binds and hurts, and — as many communications strive to convey — in fact hinders the soul's forward progress. To overcome our anguish of bereavement, we need only remind ourselves that the dead really *are* with us — and quite frequently. They can speak within our thinking and in the impulse of joy within the heart. They will not appear to us as sad ghosts outside us, but will respond to our yearning for them in a delicate and subtle way — as if we have answered the questions perplexing us within our own minds. It is through such conscious communion, such blending of thought in full awareness, that modern sensitives are able to impart to us so comprehensive a picture of the life beyond. This capacity to "tune in" to discarnate souls involves a developing of faculties which lifts us beyond communication through trance mediumship. It opens the possibility of infinitely rich and joyful relationships, in truth closer than before. Our beloved friends can indeed be "closer than breathing, nearer than hands and feet."

Unfortunately, only a limited number of people can yet really experience the subtler telepathic blending of consciousness. But we may learn from them a new outlook which can lift us courageously beyond the despair often felt, and nullify the apparent finality of loss. What we must do is open our hearts in love, transmuting the sense of tragic loss into the comfort and joy and certainty that in good time we shall be united again.

At this point, it is worth considering in more detail the phenomenon of physical death. Man consists of a physical body, the substance of which is held together by a vital body of formative forces known as the etheric. Governing these is the astral body or soul sheath, and the spirit, the eternal spiritual entity which must clothe itself in those sheaths that it may live in the density of earth. In sleep, the astral body and spirit withdraw to spiritual worlds, though few of us have sufficiently developed organs of perception to remember what transpires. In such a state, we are with our friends who have passed on, and those who have kindled their deeper faculties of perception can in fact report their experiences during sleep. This is one of the most important sources of spiritual research. The physical and etheric bodies lie on the bed unconscious, but are linked by the so-called "silver cord," by means of which the wandering soul may be instantly recalled. At that point, one awakens. In death, however, the "silver cord" is broken and no return is possible. During sleep, the etheric forces restore and energize the body. After death, the etheric body flows out and returns to the vast pool of etheric forces from which it was drawn. As it departs, the physical body begins to disintegrate. This is manifest in the changes that occur in the two days immediately after death.

Death has been called the "Great Anesthetist," for the one who is passing feels no pain. To those who watch, it may seem that the body is convulsed in a last spasm or death struggle, but the soul at this moment is rarely conscious. Certainly it is not conscious of pain. At the moment of passing, it may have a glimpse as of a passageway opening up into a dazzling light. Goethe's last words, for example, were: "Light! More light!" And William Etty, that exuberant life-loving Victorian artist, called out loudly at his last moment: "Glorious, glorious, this death!"

The ritual of lying in state for two or three days has profound meaning, for the soul during this time often hovers round its former habitation, getting accustomed to having left it. There are many descriptions of how the "dead" person finds himself floating, discarnate, above his own body. Such descriptions establish the importance of flowers around the coffin, candles and, on occasion, the vigil — as well as the necessity of avoiding fuss or frantic activity in the chamber. The astral and etheric bodies are drawn by the flowers and lights, and the process of transition is made gentler. The very stillness and dignity of the milieu aids the soul to free itself. After a time, it will probably fall into a period of unconsciousness, from which it will awaken to find itself perhaps in a beautiful "hospital" room with family or friends to greet it. As soon as it accepts the fact that it has discarded the body, that it is still very much alive, that all illness and pain has ceased, it is free to move on into a new and beautiful world. And it is at this stage that we who are left on earth can most support our departed friends by loving thoughts, sending them forth courageously on their new adventure.

"In My Father's house are many mansions," said Jesus. Many mistakenly assume that the "Summerland" is heaven. It is not. It is called, rather, the Plane of Fulfilled Desires — and also the Plane of Illusion. It is in fact but the lowest heavenly realm, infinitely rich and enjoyable though the experience found there may be. It, too, must ultimately be transcended. The soul must in time "die" again to be reborn on higher planes, until eventually it is free for soul-travel in the divine realm of pure spirit.

But it cannot do so until it is fit, and this fitness is attained through cleansing and catharsis. Each step on the journey is a more profound initiation. In her postmortem communication through Helen Greaves — transcribed in the latter's book, *Testimony of Light* — Frances Banks describes how she decided she would enter the Halls of Learning. Confidently, she strode up the steps of this temple university of the spirit, only to be thrown back by blinding light. We cannot move on to the more refined vibrations until we are sufficiently prepared for them, and in the long soul journey towards the source there are clearly many difficulties to be surmounted. All planes interpenetrate. To echo the analogy cited earlier, finer frequencies can pass through coarser ones as electromagnetic waves pass through "solid" matter. It is a question of learning how to adapt and adjust to the proper frequency, the proper vibratory rate. But the prospect of free soul travel is accessible to all of us. As we have seen, we do it in sleep, but without conscious awareness. Richelieu's remarkable book, *A Soul's Journey*, offers a description of the lifting to consciousness of this experience.

Clearly, the imperishable soul has infinite aeons for its development and exploration. The fact that earth exists as a field for experience of self-consciousness and alienation within the limitations of a gravity-bound body means that the evolving being will use this training ground a great number of times. As the whole consciousness of the earth and of mankind evolves, so the individual monad will necessarily return for further experience. It is a long education, granted. But — "Is not the whole of eternity mine?"

We have spoken of the "Summerland" and of release into light. Because the whole immense process is one of soul development and education, however, we must not assume that the higher worlds are devoid of suffering. Released from the body and the prison of the five senses, the soul is compelled to face its own limitations, inadequacies and ill-doing in the form of remorse and, not infrequently, pain. Immediately prior to the moment of death, we experience in one great flash an instantaneous panorama of our past life—a phenomenon to which those rescued from drowning, for example, bear witness. What accounts for this total recall is the release of the etheric body, which is the storehouse of memory. Subsequently, the soul passes through a long retrospective of its life, which apparently takes something like a third of the time of the actual former life span. During this retrospective, it reexperiences not only its deeds, but their consequences as well—experiences in itself, that is, the pain or pleasure it caused. What it previously visited upon others is now visited upon itself. Thus, if we were cruel to another, we would be faced with the stark realization of what our action meant by experiencing, in ourselves, its original impact on its victim. As a result, we are filled with a pain that brings understanding and remorse. Until we make such compensation, our own soul development is arrested. But compensation can be made by repentance and forgiveness on the higher plane. If the wrong in question was too grave, however, we may be obliged to incarnate again, to find the soul we once harmed and offer expiation—render some deed of sacrifice perhaps, which will redress the karmic damage and free us for further progress. This purgatorial experience is a very real one through which the soul must pass. But it is not a question of a harsh God issuing judgment. Clearly, the soul is its own and only judge, by creating situations where, within itself, it confronts the real consequences of its actions. This informs it with the urge to make amends and restitution to others, so that forgiveness may release it to advance upon its journey. We are, in short, responsible for creating our own Hell. If the soul is tethered to corporeal desires and appetites, moreover, it will suffer because in death it loses the physical organs for their satisfaction. This is the significance latent in the myth of Tantalus, forever striving to reach the grapes which are always just beyond his reach. Some souls, then, will readily put themselves through the refining fires of "Purgatory" to purify themselves of their faults and obtain access to the next stage.

To achieve this realization, we must overcome much conditioning. Our subconscious, as stated before, still bedevils us with lurid medieval pictures of Hell and Judgment. But the notion of eternal damnation is at variance with the vision which now emerges — that of the soul's self-judgment, by compassionate experience of the suffering it caused to others. It is a very primitive and simplistic view that the good or ill done in one life settles one's fate irrevocably for all eternity. Indeed, the very word "eternity" in this context is misplaced. We only move on to an "eternal" plane in the sense that it is beyond our time-space continuum of earth life. When it is fitting, we can choose to return from the higher planes into the temporal sphere for further experience and service.

Even a partial understanding of the spiritual world view serves to mitigate the fear of death which arises either from ignorance or from uncertainty about conscious survival afterwards. Modern communications are bringing to light a wonderful picture of the fields of experience after death. These offer an assurance that we do really find again those we loved and lost. If the "force field" here is gravity, that in the beyond is composed of sympathy and antipathy. We are naturally and inevitably drawn again to those with whom we have one or another kind of affinity. In this body-free realm, souls can blend and merge so that consciousness becomes one while identity is retained. Thus the experience of the ecstasy of love will be intensified, though in a subtler form than in the body. As Goethe says, everything on the temporal plane is but a parable, an image. Every earthly thing is a reflection of creative ideas and archetypes in the spiritual spheres. Thus, physical loving must be but a reflection of the glory of experience when light and love-filled souls merge on the higher planes. There need be no fear that by dying we have passed beyond the possibility of ecstasy.

Such blending of souls also provides a clue to the important principle of group souls. It is the basis on which we are drawn into a concourse of kindred spirits, amongst whom we karmically belong. It is with friends in such a group that we will incarnate again.

Though this broad vista of endless life alleviates the crude and ignorant fear of death, it does not, as stated before, mean that all life in the beyond is a rosy heavenly experience. Over the aeons, life, on whatever plane, is a continuous educational experience. Many of us, to a greater or lesser degree, will have failed to fulfil the life task and purpose for which we incarnated. We may even fail to learn what that purpose is. When in the "beyond" we recognize our failures, there may well be agonies of remorse. Though "destiny" may be "always kind," the law of cause and effect holds good, and compensation for failure and wrong-doing is inevitable. Among advanced souls who have seen these tremendous truths, there may therefore be a certain dread of death — of confronting their failure to take the steps in inner development and outer service for which they came to earth.

But knowledge of the reality of the glory of light and the imperishable nature of the soul, realization of the power of love and forgiveness, can still fill us with joy — a joy which subsumes and transforms all doubt. We can yet realize that we are individually part of a great process of evolution towards the great Oneness, while at the same time undergoing a long training — so that, as a spiritual individuality possessing free will, we can learn to become a companion of God. For man is indeed a creature

> *God begotten, God companioned*
> *Forever God-ward striving.*

Dryden called him "the Glory, jest and riddle of the world."

6 | Transformation of Man

Ultimately what we are trying to convey is the concept of a basic transformation of mankind. For every individual, this must obviously begin with his or her own self. That self is the only piece of the cosmos over which we have direct control and responsibility, and the only moment in which we can make changes with it is the fleeting "now."

All the wisdom of the East is concerned with discovering the unity of life and transcending the sense of separation, so that the smaller self may merge with the greater Self — "The droplet slips into the ocean," to quote the last line of Edwin Arnold's *Light of Asia*. As we have noted, the western mind, in contrast, possesses a much greater concern for individuality. Now, however, we are approaching the Oneness, comprehending how it sifts down through all diversity. We now see that we must somehow transmute lower self into Higher Self. Consciousness can ultimately expand to blend with the immensity of the universe; while at the same time, the paradoxical mystery and truth remains that somehow the ocean can pour itself into the drop. In meditation, we always have a focal point of consciousness, however far we lift out of the body. We are a point of light uniting with a stream of divine light, a strand of love in an ocean of love, a center of thought moving in a vast field of thought, a point of stillness or courage in a matrix of those qualities.

Steiner uses the word "ego" not as Freud does, but as a descriptive term for that entity which moves from one incarnation to another. This is the spirit, the "I" which must give itself over to the indwelling of the numinous (divine). Whatever terms we use, we must see we are striving for this alchemical transmutation within the soul, which, through the purging fire, will burn out the dross of the egoistic lower self and in time produce the gold of the soul which has accepted the I AM. This is the great evolutionary step.

Let us consider, for example, the following fragment from Francis Thompson's poem, "The Mistress of Vision":

> *Where is the land of Luthenay?*
> *Where is the tract of Elenore?*
> *I am bound therefore.*
>
> *Pierce thy heart to find the key;*
> *With thee take*
> *Only what none else would keep:*
> *Learn to dream when thou dost wake*
> *Learn to wake when thou dost sleep . . .*
> *When to the new eyes of thee*
> *All things by immortal power*
> *Near and far,*
> *Hiddenly*
> *To each other linkéd are*
> *That thou canst not stir a flower*
> *Without troubling of a star . . .*
> *Seek no more*
> *Pass the Gates of Luthenay, tread the region Elenore.*

Luthenay and Elenore are the mysterious etheric world, the land of spirit, Shamballah. The name Elenore is strangely emotive. The same sound is echoed in Alan Garner's novel, *Elidor*, where two lads from a Manchester slum break through to that world of wonder. Twice in the lines cited above the soul appeals for help in finding the way. Then, the Higher Self responds. The key lies in the injunction to "pierce thy heart," and the great secret is the knowledge, made good in experience, that we are part of the Oneness of being which underlies everything and dwells within every form. When that is "known," there is love for all being. Then the gates of Luthenay, the world of the etheric, are open. But to enter involves what T.S. Eliot describes as

> *A condition of complete simplicity*
> *Costing not less than everything.*

Now let us move on to a poem by D.H. Lawrence, which can well stand for the aspiration of each of us striving to enter the New Age, "The Song of a Man Who Has Come Through":

Not I, not I, but the wind that blows through me!
A fine wind is blowing the new direction of Time.
If only I let it bear me, carry me, if only it carry me!
If only I am sensitive, subtle, oh, delicate, a winged gift!
If only most lovely of all, I yield myself and am borrowed
By the fine, fine wind that takes its course through the chaos of the
                                                                world
Like a fine, an exquisite chisel, a wedge-blade inserted;
If only I am keen and hard like the sheer tip of a wedge
Driven by invisible blows,
The rock will split, we shall come at the wonder, we shall find the
                                                          Hesperides.
Oh, for the wonder that bubbles into my soul;
I would be a good fountain, a good well-head,
Would blur no whisper, spoil no expression.
What is the knocking?
What is the knocking at the door in the night?
It is somebody wants to do us harm.

No, no, it is the three strange angels.
  Admit them. Admit them.

It is worth examining the imagery more closely. First, there is
the wind of the spirit which can blow *through* us. The whole
being and soul can be cleansed by the wind. In meditation, we
can let it pass through the spaces that we know separate all
the circling molecules within the body — a surrender to the
wind, that we may be borrowed and used in the great catharsis
now beginning in the chaos of the world. But then Lawrence
suddenly shifts to the image of the wedge, the "exquisite chisel."
'Pierce thy heart . . .' The rock which is to be split is of course
the hardness and coldness of the lower self, encased in a materialistic outlook devoid of spirit, but the starting point is our
own heart. We have not lent ourselves to the influx of power
from the spirit unless we have begun the transformation of
man within ourselves. This involves something that can best
be described by the paradoxical phrase, "exquisite pain." So
the "exquisite chisel" splits the hardness of the rock of the
heart and, within ourselves, we come to the wonder; we find
the gateway to Elenore, the Hesperides, within us. We *are* one
with the Oneness. Furthermore, we are also the tip of the wedge.
If the hard casing of the rock of materialistic thought is to
break, it is man who must invoke the spiritual energies and
put himself at their service, becoming the point which can be
driven by the blows from the invisible worlds.

At this point, Lawrence introduces the images of well and
fountain. Each self can become a fountainhead through which
the wonder bubbles up. The soul becomes a listening organ
through which the higher world can express itself in the whisper of the "still small voice."

Finally, there is the epilogue that introduces the knocking,
at first reminiscent of the ominous hammering on the door in
the early hours of morning by the Gestapo. Yet it can also be
"He who stands at the door and knocks." May He even be

within the heart, imprisoned and knocking to get out? And the three strange angels? Surely this new impulse lifts us beyond the pattern of orthodoxy in conventional religious forms, and its messengers in consequence are indeed strange. But we must have the courage to welcome these beings. We must know that they do indeed exist.

From here, we must take another step. This transformation of man — is it not the true interpretation of resurrection? The incarnating soul truly enters a sort of grave in accepting the limitations of body and the terrible restriction of the self-seeking ego. We are the dead, "living and partly living." But "the trumpet shall sound and the dead shall be raised incorruptible and we shall be changed." Our modern minds of course reject the concept of all the rotted bodies rising. But the immortal in man takes to itself the resurrection body. "This corruptible must put on incorruption and this mortal must put on immortality." It could indeed be that "we shall be changed, in a moment, in the twinkling of an eye." Metamorphosis *is* possible.

Man can decide to throw off the fetters of his own self-bound egoistic thinking, which, when taken in mass, makes the stuff of cruder materialism. As each individual allows the rock to split and rises to the incorruptible, the fabric of the old will change and perforce a new world will appear, consecrated to glory, unity and all-encompassing Oneness.

7 | New Age Now

I<small>N THE OPENING CHAPTER</small> of this book, I made it quite clear that there is no question of trying to impose or enforce belief. We are, rather, invited to entertain new ideas, and, if we are drawn to them, to live with them until it becomes apparent whether they have the genuine ring of truth and can be accepted as integral parts of our lives. Of course the great scientists and mathematicians have often admitted that many of their discoveries have been the results of flashes of intuition coming from they knew not where. This faculty must be respected and used in our uncertain days when consciousness is breaking through into fields beyond what ordinary sense perception can attain. Since the issues involved concern the very survival of our race and of life on our planet, we are surely justified in according most serious consideration to the intuitions and communications received telepathically by sensitives all over the world, and emanating, it would appear, from higher intelligences.

In our dramatic age, we must learn to reserve judgment and keep an open mind to novel possibilities, however surprising and perhaps even unlikely they may appear at first sight. To open a chapter on the imminence of the new age, therefore, I shall quote from a lecture by Anthony Brooke, entitled "The Awakening of Man" and published in the *Findhorn News*, September, 1973. Mr. Brooke states succinctly and lucidly the human situation in its universal context:

It is evident, beyond question and beyond doubt, for all who are not entirely blind to the signs of the times, that our planet is today undergoing an acute evolutionary crisis. To the peoples of our divided world, the choice would seem to be clear — to change our ways and unite together, or to perish like the civilizations of the past.

Actually, it is not quite like that. Because while the old and outworn civilization is doomed and dying, there is already evidence of something new and glorious — a new man, a new creation — coming to birth. We are to experience this as a total healing — the welding into oneness — of our divided and tortured body of humanity.

There is, however, a need first to view our condition in its cosmic context, because we have entered into what may come to be known as the Cosmic Age — the Space Age — and I would like to offer you my understanding of what this means.

We each form part of a universe of living energy, an immense, unified field of living, pulsating energy. If we are to speak of God, then God must comprise the totality of this universal life energy and must itself be each and all of the manifestations within the universe in their countless forms, visible and invisible, and infinitely more besides, which the human mind cannot possibly comprehend. This Living Wholeness of Being is infused in its every part with a loving and purposeful intelligence and moves consistently towards maintaining itself in order, harmony and balance, towards maintaining its oneness and perfection.

It follows that man's mind is designed to be attuned, and to keep attuned, to this consciousness of oneness, of wholeness, of perfect being, and to experience this in conditions reflected in the environment, which would thus become, in metaphorical language, Heaven upon Earth. Yet we know that throughout recorded history, the very opposite has been the condition most generally experienced on earth. In the place of wholeness, perfection, order and harmony, we have tended in ourselves and in our world to experience conditions of division, imperfection, confusion and conflict, which our newspapers, television and radio daily bring to our attention.

In the urgency of the present moment, no good purpose is served by debating the reasons, associated with Man's inbuilt power of free will, why humanity throughout history has clung to an apparently self-imposed course of suffering, conflict and destruction. The important thing now for us to realize and to accept is that energies are at hand, as indeed they have always been at hand, to help us to move out of this condition.

And we cannot afford any longer to ignore them. The barriers in Man's mind are in fact today giving way to powerfully creative and uplifting energies which are flooding into his consciousness to provide him, individually and collectively, with an unparalleled opportunity to be instrumental in bringing new life to the planet, a new civilization based upon enduring values of love, truth, joy, peace and the ideal of service to his fellow human beings and to the other life-streams which contribute to and support the life of our planet. These values have been proclaimed to Man by wise ones down the ages, and now Man is required to incarnate and express them ever more consistently in his daily living if he is to enjoy any future existence upon earth. Many are the ways that are open to Man to play his part in the creative process, and these energies themselves, provided he opens himself to them, are the enabling source to provide him with the strength to be increasingly effective to this end . . .

To summarize:
1. We are being invited to accept what for many of us is a new fact, a new truth — that there are superior forms of intelligent life

in the universe which are making contact with us by various means and in various ways.

2. This intelligent life operating according to universal law and in the service of the One Supreme Universal Power is working to implement a plan for peace and brotherhood throughout the universe, which of course includes our planet.

3. The people and governments of the world can choose, individually and collectively, either to continue to strive towards a solution of the problems of the world as if our planet were an isolated unit, or we may enlarge our capacity to solve all our problems by giving recognition to, and by co-operating with, this higher wisdom and intelligence which is being made available to us.

4. We have this free choice, but higher intelligence is informing us in telepathic communications that we shall not, in fact, be able to solve the many difficulties we are continuing to create for ourselves without coming to think and live in a completely new way and without establishing an effective link, directly or indirectly, with the Higher Intelligence which governs the entire Universe. We will then be given every assistance to solve all our problems and to live a fully creative life in peace and brotherhood on earth and in harmony also with life throughout the universe.

5. In cooperation with their governments, the people of the world have a vital role to play in bringing about a universal civilization — a true brotherhood of Man upon Earth.

Most of us will surely agree that, if this picture is accurate, it offers grounds for genuine optimism. It is not theoretical talk about what might happen in the far distant future. On the contrary, all the great teachers and sensitives urge us to realize that something is really happening now. It is happening inevitably, as the barriers between the eternal and temporal planes are melted. We are witnessing the impinging of the eternal world into our plane of time. The events of which we speak represent the "intersection of the timeless with time."

The veils separating the levels of consciousness are growing very thin. The truth is that, in a most profound sense, the New Age is already here, waiting for us to bring it into manifestation by lifting and opening our awareness and allowing the timeless to be earthed. It is thus dependent on us when and where the New Age manifests. But the moment we learn how to open ourselves and invoke them, the New Age energies begin to flow. Thus man's understanding, acceptance and creative channelling is an essential factor. Just as we have noted that the higher worlds are to be found wherever we can direct our attention to them, we must also recognize that the New Age already exists. It only remains for us to determine how and where it shall assume concrete form.

As Brooke claims, there appears to be a clear intention on the part of the higher intelligences to influence man and cooperate with him wherever and whenever he offers them the opportunity. We must, however, never forget the fact that, by divine dispensation, we have been given free will. Cooperation, therefore, can never be forced, nor will it occur if we simply remain passive and wait for it. Disaster may be allowed to strike us as a salutary lesson designed to awaken us, but the true inner cooperation must await our invitation. It can come only if man calls for it in inner freedom. This, naturally, he will never do until he accepts the reality of higher worlds. Hence the importance in studying the findings of those who can research into the spiritual worlds.

The inner freedom stressed above is guaranteed by the very nature of the telepathic contact, which speaks as the "still small voice" within the mind or in the impulse to action in the heart. Though the source is all powerful, the method is delicate and gentle. Unless we can learn to still our chattering minds, we shall never hear the guidance. A spiritual being will not appear outside us and command us. It will speak telepath-ically within our thought, as if we had ourselves answered the questions we posed. In short, there is no constraint or com-pulsion. Again, we have total freedom of choice, to listen or ignore the intimation that — apparently — we offer ourselves. It is not even necessary that we know its higher source. What-ever that may be, we are continually being subtly influenced in a constructive way, for we each have our invisible guides, as well as our Higher Self. And the inner mental contact afforded by these principles is clearly the doorway to true spiritual ex-perience, lifting us beyond the dangers of deception — includ-ing the deception that rises through too great a preoccupation with psychic phenomena.

There are many qualitative degrees in the blending of minds. Those with developed intuition do really meet and converse in fullest consciousness with the beings of the spiritual worlds. Most of us, by study and rational processes, will arrive first at a recognition of the reality of these invisible forces of con-sciousness. Then we will be prepared to accept their influence and guidance. In doing so, we will implicitly acknowledge that creative intelligence is everywhere at work. And we can accept as well the concept of "living ideas" weaving through the super-sensible planes and desiring to be earthed through human thinking. In this way, we will begin to awaken to a constant and subtle penetration of our consciousness, almost like falling dew, or "dropping like the gentle rain from heaven." We must, however, admit that we are always personally responsible for what we give out. It is a mistake and a danger to say, in effect, that something was given us as a higher truth, but that we disclaim responsibility for it.

In ordinary life, man strives to solve his problems by proudly relying on his own self-sufficiency. In the New Age, this self-sufficiency must be augmented by a new cooperation, in which a man is still the fully responsible agent, yet knows that he is channelling spiritual power and accepting a measure of guidance. Only in this manner can we learn to be companions and co-creators with God — the goal of our developing sense of individuality. As Christ said to His disciples: "Hitherto I have called you servants. From now on, I shall call you friends."

The new flowering involves constant surrender of self-will and ever renewed dedication. But since freedom must always be respected, we ourselves, as stated before, must send up the invitation to our Higher Self, to enter the heart and guide our lives.

What it amounts to is a planting of the soul in the soil of the spirit, so that it may flower into new creativity. Rooted only in our lower self and personality, on the other hand, we are like a thing adrift:

> *Abide in Me, and I in you. As the branch cannot bear fruit of itself, except it abide in the vine, no more can ye except ye abide in Me.*
>
> *I AM the vine, ye are the branches. He that abideth in Me, and I in him, the same bringeth forth much fruit for without Me ye can do nothing.*
>
> *(John 15: 4,5)*

Here is the real new birth that must come about in each soul through the creative flow of the Higher Self. Here is the coming of the New Age. Uprooted, unplanted, man may drift and lose power of initiative; but once "rooted and grounded in love," he will tap new creativity. The great initiates have always demonstrated great powers of initiative, bringing spiritual power down into practical and daily life.

Once we discern the rootlessness of modern man, we can see how the psyche, in its loneliness, despair and loss of all sense of meaning, must often turn its inner drives into violence, cruelty, hate and negativity. It is a souring of human nature which has lost touch with the springs of life. To continue our analogy, it is as if the plant of the soul is being fed only with artificial fertilizers and sprayed with poisons. What it needs instead is to be set again in living humus and re-united with the cycle of life.

The flow of new age energies must inevitably draw kindred souls into new groupings, the focal points of a new society. Where the living spirit floods the consciousness, values cannot but change, and we shall wake up to the significance of things we have hitherto taken for granted. Thus, certain practices now accepted in our present-day society will simply fall away and fade out of new age culture as it begins to coalesce. Let us take a single example. Once we really recognize our kinship with all life, we shall cease to be able to take life. Cruelty to animals will become intolerable. Such hideous practices as factory farming and vivisection will be revealed for the barbarities they truly are and will be abandoned. To engage in blood sports for pleasure will become unthinkable; and, for more and more people, the eating of once living flesh will become abhorrent. We shall then awaken to the fact that we have an immense karmic debt to the animal world, and that until this is settled, man's spiritual progress will be retarded. The movement for animal welfare has a profound significance in human collective destiny.

Since the New Age involves a fundamental transformation in the very nature of man, we may expect killing and violence — so prevalent today — to wane. Gandhi's vision of nonviolence will become an ever greater reality, and in the end war will be universally recognized as the insanity it intrinsically is.

The basic virtues of tolerance, honesty, respect for truth, cooperation and compassion will become ever more manifest, while the very capacity to deceive another, to bear false witness, steal or murder will be eradicated from the patterns of human behavior.

We are not talking about naive optimism, pious hopes or airy idealism. Certainly it is idealistic, yet at the same time it is practicable and intensely relevant to daily life. The New Age is not a social plan based on intellectual concepts. It is a living impulse which, by its very nature, carries transforming power. Once it begins to touch the soul, a person will inevitably begin to change. And the impulse will spread rapidly, drawing more and more people into its field of influence, for it is nothing less than a mystical event of which we are all the potential instruments. The wind of the spirit blows through us. It transcends and subsumes the cynicism that might point out the cruelty and violence so characteristic of our age. We are talking about a *new* society which is now emerging through a metamorphosis of the old. "Let Light and Love and Power restore the Plan on Earth."

The present situation is well summarized in a quotation from a lecture by David Spangler, author of a most important little book entitled *Revelation: the Birth of a New Age:*

> *A new world is taking birth. This world already exists and in a sense, its energies are precipitating out into form.*
>
> *People throughout the world are beginning to attune to this energy, because in their higher consciousness they are already part of that world. They are citizens of it, though they may not know it consciously. Through the power of their lives, in their individual and collective demonstration, they provide precipitation points.*
>
> *As this new world increases in vitality, the world that has vitalized form up to this point will decrease in vitality and will, in a manner of speaking, fade away.*
>
> *This transition between two worlds could be smooth or could be chaotic, according to the will of the individuals involved. As far as the energies of the new world are concerned, the change has already taken place and there was no destruction. There was*

only the opportunity to join with a Divine energy, to become a co-creator of a new planet.

The path is an adventure into the unknown which is at the same time a return to the source, with the certainty that we all have loving and invisible guides to help us overcome the difficulties and trials of the way. It involves a conscious building of soul qualities. This in turn entails a deliberate and creative deed, for we recognize that when we sound a quality in the soul, it resounds or reverberates up onto higher planes. Just as a note struck on the piano evokes a resonance on higher octaves, so we may expect a response to that which is sounded in our souls. We may then see that the spiritual worlds are in a sense composed of living qualities and attributes which are also Being. Thus we can grasp that courage is an attribute of the sphere of Mars, joviality of Jupiter, steadfastness of Saturn. In meditation, we leave our everyday consciousness and enter into absolute tranquility. At this moment, we are poised in the "eternal now" at the "intersection of the timeless with time." Regret for the past or anxiety about the future is simply nonexistent. The negative emotions of the lower self are for this precious timeless moment in total abeyance, and the soul can consciously sound the qualities which it discerns the Higher Self to possess. These are basically peace and tranquility, love, courage, joy, and gentleness. By sounding them, we evoke the higher response and the character is strengthened. When we plunge back into daily life, we will be suffused and colored by those positive qualities, as if the soul had been dipped into a dye.

In sum, then, we can indeed *"take courage."* It is a highly significant phrase. To touch the plane of attributes and qualities is truly a creative act. Take joy, take love, take peace, take the lot! It is your birthright, your heritage. As ambassadors of the divine, it is our assignment and task to re-enter life with positive thinking for active transformation of our environments. Thus, each can contribute to the birth of the New Age. Each human being and each group is potentially a vortex point through which spiritual quality can flood. Arithmetic is irrelevant here. A small breach in a dam can lead to a flood. A small group can channel energies which, once released, will take their own course, since they are imbued with intelligence, life and love. Our task is to dedicate ourselves as channels, to invoke the higher energies and, with praise, to give thanks. Then we must go forward living into the new day, with joy and courage.

Messages and communications received by sensitives — as recorded, for example, in the book *Gildas Communicates*, by Ruth White and Mary Swainson — speak of inevitable changes as the new energies begin to flow. These changes would obviously imply a radical change in consciousness. Many people would begin to see with fourth or fifth dimensional vision. Others, fettered to a materialistic perspective, might feel they were going mad. And there might be changes in the outer world as well, in climate and even geological disturbances. This might be construed by some as the retribution to be visited upon man for his treatment of the living earth. Yet the teachers from the world of spirit all urge us to have no fear. Indeed, "fear not" is always the first injunction of the spiritual visitant. Disaster and calamity may serve a purpose for the higher worlds — to awaken man to the evil of his ways. We may feel confident that the more difficult outer conditions become, the closer and more certain will be the individual protection and assistance of our invisible guides. New dimensions of knowledge are being opened up, and the new age vision will clarify and crystallize as living ideas work to counter the collapse of antiquated forms.

Of course it is quite impossible in so brief a book as this to do justice to what is now so rapidly emerging, or, in Spangler's phrase, "precipitating." Suffice it to say at this point that it is occurring on an ever broader scale. In centers and communes, in meditation and healing groups, in conferences and lectures, in yoga teaching, in courses and activities offered by the great schools of esoteric knowlege, in international contacts, in the striving of individuals for higher knowledge, in books and publications and the creative and performing arts — everywhere, the vast vista of the ageless wisdom unfolds. It is indeed to be seen as one of the truly significant phenomena in the intellectual climate of our time.

In light of this picture, we might consider what the so-called "rebellion of youth" really means. In doing so, we must remember that there is no death without a rebirth and that human society is like every new growth in nature, involving first a breaking down of matter into sheer formlessness or chaos, as in the seed. Chaos or formlessness is the necessary precursor to new birth on a higher level. We must now apply this principle to what we are witnessing about us — the disturbance of an entire generation, many rejecting all old forms, opting out of accepted standards, experimenting with previously forbidden directions, deliberately breaking sacrosanct taboos. Youth in revolt, in quest — for what?

If our earlier premise is true, many of these souls chose to descend into the maelstrom of world affairs so as to be at their full maturity at the time of the coming spiritual crisis. Many are no doubt advanced and mature souls who chose the task of leading the new society into social forms consonant with the spirit. They came with a task, but the nature of life on earth is such that we forget wholly the wider vision we witnessed from the heavenly planes before descent into birth. What, then, do these old souls incarnate as young people find? They are confronted with gross materialism, values based on greed and selfishness and aggression, a rejection of love, a scramble for possession of things and power. And quite naturally, they revolt, because no parent or mentor has reminded them that there exists a wholly different perspective, which affords a view of man as a spiritual being, an ambassador of God, given responsibility for the stewardship of this lovely planet, enjoying the possibility of cooperation with the power of light and love in starting to build a new order on earth. Without such a perspective, it is not surprising that many are adrift and lost. If this is indeed the soul condition of many of the younger generation, we may expect an instant response when the spiritual world view is rendered accessible to them. All they need is to be reminded.

Bewildered as many now are, experimenting blindly with drugs, for example, in their quest to escape from the cage of self, these young people will in a sudden flash recollect and half remember the task they undertook and the vistas they witnessed before they entered their present "trial by existence." Then, when spiritual change begins, when the powers of light descend, these young people — already freed from all binding ties of convention — will be in a position to rise to the call of "Follow me!" They will know and understand. For this they came. Then all that now seems negative may turn into positive creation, and above and beyond our present social structure a new society will begin to form, based truly on love and immediate contact with the divine sources of guidance. The prospect is exhilarating. With all its apparent darkness and confusion, this is truly an age of joy, and Schiller's "Hymn to Joy," echoed in Beethoven's 9th Symphony, should indeed be its anthem — along with Blake's "Jerusalem."

Never before has man lived through an age so pregnant with promise, and we must acknowledge that many of the young in our time are souls who have chosen to be involved with the greatest surge forwards in spiritual evolution that the human race has ever experienced. Such are the days in which we live, and they are bright with the most supreme hope ever offered to struggling and troubled man.

> *Awake, awake, the world is young*
> *For all its weary years of thought,*
> *The starkest fights must still be fought,*
> *The most surprising songs be sung.*
> *—James Elroy Flecker*

William Blake, who really wrote less for his own time than for ours, sounded the apocalyptic clarion call: "RISE UP, YOUNG MEN OF THE NEW AGE!" This is, of course, high-sounding and idealistic stuff, easily written. Yet in a world of as much darkness and conflict as ours, set apparently on a course of collective suicide through unbalanced materialism, it may well be worthwhile making the last cast of banking all on a world view which, if true, offers an optimistic alternative. At this turning point in human affairs, we have so little to lose, and eternity to gain.

Of course the personal and social difficulties confronting us are huge and daunting. To live in an apocalyptic age is exciting, but not particularly comfortable, not conducive to a desire for either psychological or material security. But once we grasp the tremendous possibilities that extend all the way down into practical life, we can face all trials and tribulations. And we can do so with the zest of members of a resistance movement awaiting an invasion for which warning has already been sounded. If many of our young have "dropped out" of our acquisitive society, it is perhaps an unconscious prelude to a step forwards into a new one — of which courage, love and joy are the basic ingredients, once heart and mind are kindled with the fire of the living spirit.

It will be appropriate to close this chapter with a quotation from Sri Aurobindo, published in the Auroville magazine, " = One." We must remember that this is a call to the young in heart, however many years they may have lived, for the soul within us is immortal and ageless.

OUR CALL IS TO THE YOUNG

The future belongs to the young.
It is a young and new world which is now under process of
    development
and it is the young who must create it.

*But it is also a world of truth, courage, justice, lofty aspirations
    and straightforward fulfillment*
which we seek to create.
Our ideal is a new birth of humanity into the spirit;
our life must be a spiritually inspired effort
to create a body of action for the great new birth and creation.
Our ideal is not the spirituality that withdraws from life
but the conquest of life by the power of the spirit.
It is to accept the world as an effort of manifestation of the Divine,
but also to transform humanity
by a greater effort of manifestation than has yet been accomplished,
one in which the veil between man and God shall be removed,
the divine manhood of which we are capable shall come to birth
*and our life shall be remolded in the truth and light and power of
    the spirit.*
It is the young who are free in mind and heart
to accept a completer truth and labor for a greater ideal.
*They must be men and women who will dedicate themselves not
    to the past or the present*
but to the future.
*They will need to consecrate their lives to an exceeding of their
    lower self,*
to the realization of God in themselves and in all human beings
*and to a whole-hearted and indefatigable labor for the nation and
    for humanity.*
*This ideal can be as yet only a little seed and the life that embodies
    it a small nucleus,*
but it is our fixed hope that the seed will grow into a tree
and the nucleus be the heart of an ever-extending formation.
*It is with a confident trust in the spirit that inspires us that we take
    our place*
*among the standard-bearers of the new humanity that is struggling
    to be born.*

8 | Living into Change

ALVIN TOFFLER, a professor of futuristic sociology, contends in his *Future Shock* that when the demands of social and personal adjustment are too great, a psychological state occurs in which people become incapable of decision and initiative. We might conceive of this state as a species of soul-paralysis — an instinctive protest against the pressure of inordinate demands. We have spoken before of the imminence of tremendous changes. If Toffler's argument is valid, it is then of paramount importance to train ourselves to move into conditions for which we have no precedent and without being thrown off poise or out of balance.

It is certainly sufficiently apparent that mankind is approaching a great spiritual crisis or turning point, a partial consequence of its entry into the Aquarian Age. The seers and adepts of our time foresee profound inner changes before the end of the century. As we have mentioned, these may involve, for many people, the opening of fourth and fifth dimensional awareness. And the higher worlds are deeply concerned with what happens on this planet. They are prepared to pour in the powers of light for the redemption of mankind — but only if a sufficient number of men will invoke them and call on them to descend.

In considering how to face change, therefore, we must learn how to open our consciousness to spiritual forces which can work creatively within us. This is the supreme challenge and hope. Using it as a basic foundation, we may train ourselves to live into the new without succumbing to "future shock" or losing psychic balance.

In considering "living into change," we must first and foremost make good the oft-repeated aphorism that only the present moment exists. The past is dead, the future may never come as we expect it. The Eternal Now is the one moment over which we have control and in which we can make changes. Yet this moment too is instantly past. It is a razor edge of moving experience. Like a surf rider, we are poised on the surging crest of an advancing wave. If we lose balance, we are thrown back to flounder in the backwash of memories and remorse for the past, or forward into a turmoil of anxieties about a future that may never come.

> Oh my Beloved, fill the Cup that clears
> Today of past regrets and future fears.

Fitzgerald's translation of the *Rubaiyat* is only ostensibly and superficially in praise of "drinking and being merry for tomorrow we may die." Seen more profoundly, it is an allegorical statement of eternal value. It speaks of the wine of life and the Cup offered by Him who called Himself the "True Vine." In *God Calling*, one passage given from the high source reads as follows:

> *Regret nothing. Not even the sins and failures. Man is so made that he can carry the weight of twenty-four hours — no more. Directly he weighs down with the years behind and the days ahead, his back breaks. I have promised to help you with the burden of today only; the past I have taken from you, and if you, foolish hearts, choose to gather again that burden and bear it, then, indeed, you mock Me to expect Me to share it. For weal or woe each day is ended. What remains to be lived, the coming twenty-four hours, you must face as you awake.*

A man on a march on earth carries only what he needs for that march. Would you pity him if you saw him bearing too the overwhelming weight of the worn-out boots and uniforms of past marches and years? And yet, in the mental and spiritual life, man does these things. Small wonder My poor world is heartsick and weary. Not so must you act.

We must admit, if we are honest, that the present moment, in all its actuality, is rarely intolerable. Our agonies are nearly all associated with regrets and remorse about the past or worries about what might happen in a week, a month, a year. "One step enough for me," as Newman said. We are metaphorically crossing a morass on stepping stones in a fog. The next step is always apparent to us, but no more. Our fears arise from looking too far ahead. Once we implant in our soul the certainty that we are each of us led by invisible guides who have an overall view above the fog, we may step forwards boldly.

Our spiritual world view does bring this certainty and it is essential to brave living into change. The invisible worlds *do* exist. Each man's destiny *is* guided by beneficent mentors. There *are* angels who watch our faltering footsteps and are there to help and serve. Once we accept this, we *can* step forwards with courage into the unknown, which is *not* unknown to our Higher Self. If the invisible helpers are not allowed to exist for us, however, we will truly flounder in uncertainty, driven to cling desperately to old fixed modes, habits and thought forms.

We have stressed that we are living in apocalyptic days. We must expect changes — social, psychological and even in the outer world. Many think that man's treatment of the living earth has been such that this great sentient being will strike back in protest. Whether that be literally true or not, we are in any case in an epoch for which we have no precedent in history. What then should we do? Often we feel helpless and revert to brain tracks or habits which lead us back into old anachronistic reactions and an opportunity is therefore thrown away. How often we "kick ourselves" for doing this! But how *do* we move forwards into change? One clue may lie with the Chinese, in whose language there is no word for "crisis." The closest Chinese approximation is "opportunity for important decisions."

Our world view, as we have seen, includes the principle of the Higher Self. Each of us has this "utterly trustworthy parental being," to use the "Huna" phrase, who is part of the super-conscious world and a counterpart to our subconscious mind. Psychology as yet is only beginning to recognize this all-important factor in our being, though it appears to be the source of many of the creative impulses in our conduct previously explained as sublimation of the sexual drive. What we are really working with are higher "drives," issuing from the light-filled plane of the superconscious, and the Higher Self is our Higher Ego into which our lower ego must in time be dissolved. If we can accept this postulate, we can proceed to act upon it. And literally "act." For we *can* act into our Higher Self. Faced with a crisis situation that lacks all precedent, we can in a flash of lifted imagination conceive how our Higher Self would react and then bravely *act the part*. This is a valid and creative use of the inherent power of acting which resides in all of us. It opens up a new field for the sublimated actor latent in everyone. We can move beyond the amateur drama club and carry the same talents, through conduct established on the creative imagination, into the kingdom of the Higher Self. Then we may learn to move into change with the certainty that we are indeed being guided, even through totally unprecedented circumstances.

The trouble is that, when faced with a sudden call to action, we frequently allow a preconception to flash into our minds which then determines our course of conduct. Once this occurs, there is little hope for a new course, since the preconception must perforce throw us back into an already experienced habit.

Thus we must learn to inhibit the instant reaction to the stimulus of the event and calmly review the available alternatives and options, using the imagination to feel out the new. This is one aspect of what Keats called "Negative Capability" — "that is, that a man is capable of being in uncertainties, mysteries and doubts, without any irritable reaching after fact and reason." As the poet contends, it is this quality that goes to make a man of achievement.

As an analogy, we might consider a fencing match or duel. We may be faced with some challenge — which perhaps we take as insult and which kindles our anger. We hit back, parry and riposte, with bitter words — or worse. But this is just what "the devil" wishes, and draws us down into painful emotion and mutual injury. On the other hand, we can, if we choose, parry the attack but recognize that the true riposte is not at our opponent but at our own lower-self reaction. Outer circumstances are so frequently the counterpart of our inner world. If we can inhibit the harmful reaction and bring our emotional response under control, we are free to choose a reaction which does no damage.

As we have stated, our inner world and our outer world are closely linked. We all have flaws in our characters which actually draw us into situations and circumstances — usually involving people — which present us with the temptation to "fall" anew. As long as such weaknesses are not overcome, we will succumb to the temptation again and again. Through agony, we at last recognize what is happening and by creative and imaginative conduct can learn to use the temptation itself to overcome the flaw. John Vyvyan, in his book *Shakespearean Ethic*, develops this principle as an important key to the understanding of Shakespeare's tragedies. The protagonist is confronted by the temptation which is the counterpart of the flaw in his character, falls, and is thrown into mental and emotional confusion; he is then hit a second time, and if he falls again the situation deteriorates to the point where the stage is littered with corpses. If the act of creative mercy can intervene, however, there is hope for redemption.

As a result of the materialistic foundation of our science, we are too prone to assume that character is solely the product of heredity and environment. This affords us the convenient excuse to transfer responsibility for how we behave to an external cause — one's parents were separated, one was an only child, one's family was too poor, one's environment was intolerable . . . But the whole picture can be reversed. My "I" is an eternal being. Therefore, "I" was already a developed soul before I was born. Indeed, I must logically have used this earth plane many times previously in the long evolution of my soul. Therefore, in cooperation with my Higher Self and spiritual guides, I must have been given some form of preview of the destiny I was assuming when I decided to incarnate.

If we can accept this view, it offers a new courage and involves a shouldering of ultimate responsibility. It implies that *we truly are the total cause* of all that we are and all that happens to us. There are really no accidents, because our Higher Self stages situations and experiences which are essential for our inner progress. Seen from the spiritual perspective, we *choose* our heredity and environment as the outward setting for experiences and circumstances which may develop the inner man. If we are really courageous, we will act on the assumption that we took on the task of transmuting a difficult environment. The frontier pioneer in the American West took pride in tackling and taming wild country. So we may feel that we have taken upon ourselves a task in descending into a difficult and intricate web of circumstances. But it is in their very difficulty and intricacy that they present a challenge for redemption and transformation — which, if we prove worthy of it, enables us to serve the world and mankind.

We must, moreover, face the implications of this heavenly preview of our destiny before descending to the "obscuration upon earth." We know that, since mankind is approaching a great spiritual turning point, the next twenty years are critically important. A great many souls must be crowding into incarnation that they may be present to experience the great events of this generation. If we have awakened to these implications and set our feet on the path to spiritual understanding, we may be sure that each of us, in his or her present incarnation, has a special task, however humble. We incarnated by intent and with a purpose, and probably in association with a group of souls with whom we have been together in previous earth lives. For the moment, we have perhaps forgotten the original task. But our Higher Self still knows it, and waits patiently for us to recall it. When we do so, when we see and acknowledge what we are meant to fulfill before we leave this plane, a new meaning and sense of purpose will be imparted to our lives. We will then be able to go forward into battle with greater certainty and courage, working in ever greater consciousness with our Higher Self. The spiritual movement in our society may be expected to develop with ever greater momentum and purpose as individual souls learn to recognize the task they undertook in coming to birth. Furthermore, as ever increasing numbers of workers for the spirit move on to the higher planes, we may expect ever closer cooperation. The New Age groups are continually being strengthened by their members who, released from bodily limitations, can work in the subtle blending of thought from the soul world.

We must have faith enough to see what it means to start absolutely from where we are now. For *we are where we are meant to be.* This is axiomatic once we admit to our invisible guides. If we are striving for understanding of the spirit, we must assume we are now where "they" want us. We are all volunteers in an army which takes no conscripts. If the "High Command" wishes to post us somewhere else, our Higher Self — a part of that Command — will have no difficulty staging events and circumstances which transport us out of our present condition and into the one desired. Again, however, we must act on this courageous view that we *are* in the right place now and the more consciously we recognize the "guidance," the more positive and remarkable it will become. In the meantime, we float in our little canoes down a great river of events. If we fight against the current, we court disaster. If—with real trust—we let ourselves go with that current, we can negotiate a path through the immediate wild water. We have no time to think about or be concerned with the rapids far ahead.

If it is true that we choose our lives and are being guided through experience on the earth plane of "separation," it is axiomatic that we must have inherent soul powers to overcome all difficulties. The spiritual pattern truly suggests that we *must* have latent reserves of strength on which we can draw to overcome any obstacle, and every such triumph further strengthens the soul for the next step in the adventure.

Each man is truly an ambassador of the divine. We descend by intent into the chaos of the world and are each responsible for our personal areas of growth and activity. Thus when we pray "Thy Kingdom come on earth," we are in one sense referring to ourselves—to our particular place of "earth," represented by all the ramifications of connection, responsibility and activity which constitute our life at the moment. In all these factors, we are backed and supported by the invisible guides so that nothing happens purely by chance. When life is considered from a broader perspective, there are few, if any, accidents. The events which seem to us accidents are in fact staged by our invisible guides to enable us to take a further step in development. "To him that overcometh will be given the crown." At any rate, to *act as if* all accidents and untoward events were planned for us by or through our Higher Self develops in us a strong and courageous view of our lives. We will not whine or complain if we shoulder full responsibility for all we are and all that happens to us. We are total cause. History is us and now.

A most constructive change of attitude accompanies this sort of thinking. It diverts us from excessive preoccupation with our own petty wills. If our plans go awry and we are prevented from doing what we wished, our attitude will not be disappointment or resentment, but rather a serious reappraisal of what is required of us and what new door has opened. Thus daily life will become increasingly an exploration into the ever new, with continuous opportunity for free choice and, simultaneously, an awareness of higher guidance. On earth we are learning to be free moral beings and to exercise creative initiative. For this, man has come into incarnation. We move out of the age of aggrandizement by the self-conscious ego into the New Age of transforming that ego into an instrument that can, in freedom, say: "Thy Kingdom come, Thy will be done . . ." But man does not simply wait on divine grace. He must rise to the obligation imposed upon him, to become co-creator and take the initiative in forming a new society in cooperation with higher worlds of being. Hence, "living into change" is the great creative task for all of us.

Most of us have reached a stage of evolution that precludes our indulging in brutality or other excesses born of animal passions. Most of the things we do which hurt others are errors of judgment, which may have to be made good by agonies of remorse. "Seven times tried that judgment is — That did never choose amiss." In other words, our wrongdoing is usually more the mistakes of the reasoning middle self than the passions of the instinctual animal lower self. To illustrate a correlative of this principle, it is worth considering a passage of *Little Gidding*, in which Eliot speaks of the "gifts reserved for age":

> . . . *the rending pain of re-enactment*
> *Of all that you have done and been; the shame*
> *Of motives late revealed, and the awareness*
> *Of things ill done and done to others harm*
> *Which once you took for exercise of virtue.*

Then fools' approval stings and honor stains.
From wrong to wrong the exasperated spirit
Proceeds, unless restored by that refining fire
Where you must move in measure, like a dancer.

Here indeed is the secret: the passage into the Now is like a dance, and we can voluntarily give ourselves to the refining fire. This fire is the remorse, disappointment, desire of atonement or agony of loss, into which we may plunge until it purges and purifies us. It will be sloughed when the soul lesson is learned, for we will realize ultimately that all loss on this plane is recompensed on the higher planes after death. There we shall meet again those we thought we had lost, in conditions that allow us to blend much more closely than we ever could in embodiment. Then there will arise the opportunity to do those things our life on earth did not, for one reason or another, permit. We must forego so much in the limitation of a body, while in the hereafter we can move into realms of freer creative action. The blending of inner world and outer world makes our passage through events like a dance. We can let go into it and accept what comes in each day. For we are to experience the metamorphosis of the soul through the refining fire, a burning away of the dross as we move into the flame in conscious acceptance.

Whenever one permits oneself to express discouragement, criticism, cynicism, anger or fear, one sends out a jet of darkness into the already darkened psychic atmosphere of the world — which, in consequence, rebounds back on us to our own further detriment. Conversely, whenever one takes the initiative and attempts to build high-self positive qualities into the soul, one strengthens the bond with the planes of light. This is our human duty and purpose. It has been contended that we are the vocabulary we use. We are obviously free to choose to cut out all negative expressions. If we allow none such to pass our lips, we will in time eradicate them from our thoughts as well. We can, in short, learn to use what has been called "the perfect language."

Meditation is a channel for continuous reconstitution of the self, to prepare it that it may move into the new. Our lower self is a creature of habit, repeating brain tracks from the unconscious. These must frequently be expunged so that we may allow new impulses from the Higher Self. In the daily period of meditation, we achieve the inner stillness and tranquility necessary for this purpose. The entire nervous system and the vital processes rest as in deep sleep, while there is a condition of alert attention in the mind, a listening to the world of being. We are then open to the qualities of the Higher Self, which essentially are peace, love, gentleness, courage and joy.

While these fill the soul, there is simply no room for the negative qualities of the lower self, which include remorse, regret, disappointment, anger, resentment for things past, and fear, anxiety and doubt about the future. These negative emotions cannot enter, any more than darkness can remain in a room when we switch on the light.

When we pray that we be forgiven our trespasses, we may regard that "us" as the partnership of the low self with the conscious middle self personality. Forgive, in other words, the silly things and blunders and hurts of which "we" were guilty yesterday. Let the mirror be wiped clean so that today we may start afresh and try again. This the Higher Self is always prepared to do. Indeed, in a real sense, the self *is* new each day. The self who thought itself insulted a week ago no longer exists. I now live afresh in a new dawn. Once I see this, I know not only that "to understand all is to forgive all," but truly that "there is nothing to forgive," for each day, once we see it, constitutes a new start, a new reality. Polish the mirror afresh and reflect the positive Higher Self qualities.

One means of teaching the lower self to be still and tranquil is, as we have noted, meditation. In meditation, we receive an intimation of the joy and bliss of being in touch with the higher qualities. Then, when we plunge back into the day's activities, all our doings will increasingly be colored by the positive impulses. Each day, in fact, they are so strengthened, and the citadel in the soul becomes more powerful, more impregnable to the transitory assaults of the phenomenal world. But the lower self must be trained to defend this citadel against attack by darker thoughts or impulses. In this way, we can build a sanctuary of light in heart and mind which gradually can be held intact throughout the day's ordeals. And in time, the whole day itself becomes a continuous meditation — "the yoga of action." The citadel will then indeed become impregnable. If it is filled with light, we will indeed have made our real contribution to the coming of the New Age. As Jesus says, "If I be lifted up, all men will be lifted with me." Each in his small way must work towards this end.

The image of the citadel is particularly apt, and it is worth developing further. For we are each involved in the war against the powers of darkness. Each of us is a spearhead or bridgehead in the great battle now being joined between light and spirit on the one hand, and, on the other, the dragon of materialistic and negative thinking. In Goethe's *Faust*, Mephistopheles introduces himself as "Ich bin der Geist der stets verneint." — "I am the Spirit (or Principle) which denies (or negates or invalidates or withers) everything." He is the vitiator, the repudiation of the spirit, the eternal negative of cold mocking laughter. We must fight him by commitment, by positive thinking and action. And we *can* do so, backed and supported as we are by the forces of light, which long, through our initiative, to subsume and redeem the earth plane.

We might — if it does not sound too presumptuous — compare ourselves to the Theban army in ancient Greece. It was an army made up of companions, of lovers. In the front rank fought the young man, immediately backed by his older friend; and both were certain that, through the love each bore the other, neither would succumb to cowardice. So we can feel

ourselves backed and supported in the fight by the Invisible
Lover, who is our Higher Self. To quote from Mabel Collins'
book, *Light on the Path:*

> *Look for the Warrior and let him fight in thee. Obey him, for*
> *he is thyself, yet infinitely wiser than thyself . . . Then thou canst*
> *go through the fight cool and unwearied, standing aside and letting*
> *him battle for thee. Then it will be impossible for you to strike one*
> *blow amiss. But if you look not to him, if you pass him by, then*
> *there is no safeguard for thee. Thy brain will reel, and thy heart*
> *grow uncertain in the dust of the battlefield. He is thyself. Yet thou*
> *art but finite and liable to error; he is eternal and is sure. He is*
> *eternal truth. When once he has entered thee and become thy*
> *warrior, he will never utterly desert thee; and at the day of the*
> *great peace, he will become one with thee.*

If we can really make our inner citadel impregnable and so
advance into battle, we will achieve something of immeasurable importance. We will have created a seed point in the soul
which we will carry through into the life between death and
rebirth. Then, when the time comes for the ego to reincarnate,
it can, with this strengthened seed, draw to itself improved
quality in the astral body or soul, and enter earth life again
with much bad Karma erased and expunged. We are truly working for the future of our own souls and that of the planet as a
whole. We are involved in an endless process of metamorphosis
of the soul as a creative deed, which assumes ever greater interest and significance as we awaken to what it implies.

Something like a new moral principle is emerging in our age.
For the Victorian mind, "obeying conscience" and "doing the
right thing" rendered all issues quite clear. "Budge, says the
fiend. Budge not, says my conscience." Now, however, things
are rarely so cut and dried, rarely so simplistically black and
white. On the contrary, they are fraught with a new and often
terrifying complexity. We are constantly offered a multitude

of ways, each of which may in all likelihood lead to injury or difficulty. And we must deliberately choose, incurring the karmic consequences, whatever they may be. As if we were mountain-climbing, a number of routes open before us and we must choose one, putting the rejected alternatives out of mind and not looking back with regret. Positive thinking often calls for selection of the boldest and most exciting, most dynamic course. For most of us, if we look back, the most profound regrets are for what we failed to do, for the opportunities missed. The gush of impulse in the heart suggests a course of action — but then, how often, we allow cold intellect to divert us, to dampen our intention, to rationalize us into paralysis. It would cost too much, people might think us silly, we have an appointment.

> *Thus conscience doth make cowards of us all*
> *And thus the native hue of resolution*
> *Is sicklied o'er with the pale cast of thought*
> *And enterprises of great pith and moment*
> *With this regard their currents turn away*
> *And lose the name of action.*

In this respect, we are all like Hamlet. But when we acknowledge guidance and direction from the Higher Self, we see that it speaks precisely in the impulse of the heart or the flash in the mind or the still small inner voice. So quiet, so discreet and unobtrusive are these hints that we too easily miss them, and they are overlaid by our chattering intellects and hard cold reasoning. Yet we *can* learn to work with this subtle cooperation. It is truly the key to "living into change." Self-deception is of course easy. Obviously we cannot blindly trust all our heart impulses — which may not ultimately be issuing from the heart at all. But we can accept that we are learning to use a telepathic contact with the Higher Self, our guide, who must speak delicately. Again, there is no constraint, no enforcement. But the technique for exploration of the New is clear.

We are indeed learning to work with our INNER TEACHER. This may be of paramount importance for New Age education. Much education today is composed of learning information imposed from without, of cold facts, statistics and data. Such things may have little relevance for wholly new conditions in the future. What we most need for "living into change" is a method of contacting our inner teacher. As Browning says in his poem, "Paracelsus":

> *Truth is within ourselves: it takes no rise*
> *From outward things, whate'er we may believe.*
> *There is an inmost center in us all*
> *Where Truth abides in fullness: and around*
> *Wall upon wall, the gross flesh hems it in,*
> *That perfect clear perception—which is truth.*
> *A baffling and perverting carnal mesh*
> *Binds it, and makes all error: and, to KNOW,*
> *Rather consists in opening out a way*
> *Whence the imprisoned splendor may escape,*
> *Than in effecting entry for a light*
> *Supposed to be without.*

We must, therefore, devise forms of training that will facilitate contact with the inner sources of truth. Then, with ever greater confidence, we will find we can move through into the unknown. The greater the spiritual crisis, the more certainly will the higher world offer its guidance and protection to those who are dedicated to its service. Therefore, in the ultimate apocalyptic challenge, we must be prepared to commit ourselves wholly to the new.

We are moving into a New Age, which on inner planes is with us already. The advent of this New Age means axiomatically that to the spirit all things are possible. In the spirit (Oneness) is abundance. And here we touch a new economic law for a new society. For Oneness can obviously answer all needs. At present, we spend our lives working less to satisfy needs than to satisfy wants and desires. Wants and desires are very different from genuine needs. If we could really learn to work for the latter, however, they would be supplied as if miraculously. Numerous groups and individuals have demonstrated the truth of this statement, particularly in our time. It entails, however, an abandonment of which most of us are incapable — until extremity compels us to have recourse wholly to it. Then the "miracles" can begin to occur. What is necessary is a sort of reckless reliance on the divine. When this act of trust can be performed, it will produce results. It entails, as we have noted, a surrender of self-will, but it does not entail becoming an ascetic. "Leave all and follow me" can mean simply a total casting away of the past with all its failures or successes, and a completely new beginning in the daily present. We must learn to "think abundance" and to know that all things are possible.

Our collective Higher Self is building a new world, right down into material society, and it wants nothing but the highest quality on all levels. We need not feel we are called to an arid Puritanism, which is often associated with readiness to accept the second-rate. The spirit is Cavalier enough to appreciate, and insist upon, the most colorful and beautiful, the very best.

Cavalier and Puritan represent the great cleavage in modern British history and collective character. We each of us carry the polarity between them in our very souls. According to *1066 & All That*, "the Roundheads were right but repulsive and the Cavaliers were wrong but romantic." A basic, if only partial truth! Puritanism knew that the new consciousness must rise above the sensual, but it seared and withered the soul by its sterile aridity. The Cavaliers, though lapsing at times into excessive licentious enjoyment, simultaneously delighted in ritual and beauty. It may be that the New Age is beginning to resolve this basic cleavage in the national character. Certainly we are lifting above the lower sensual to a realization of the subtler senses, which brings a deeper and more refined delight — as well as a demand for beauty in form and ritual living. We are also rediscovering the romance and idealism inherent in reality, for never was there a more poetic or beautiful vision of new possibilities for transforming all that is sordid in our lives. Thus the Puritan in us rises above the downward drag of the coarser senses and unites with the true Cavalier in our nature, which longs for joy in life, beauty, and color of ever new forms. *Quality* is necessary for the New Age. Everything is to be the best on every level, but there is to be nothing beyond what is necessary. Thus we must be able to *simplify* in our lives, while at the same time to strive for beauty, trusting absolutely that prayers will be answered which are tendered for the satisfaction of genuine needs.

Let us close this chapter with a little poem by T.E. Brown called "Indwelling." It summarizes the whole issue with exquisite brevity:

> *If thou coulds't empty all thyself of self*
> *Like to a shell dishabited*
> *Then might He find thee on an ocean shelf*
> *And say: 'This is not dead'*
> *And fill thee with Himself instead.*
>
> *But thou art so replete with very thou*
> *And hast such shrewd activity*
> *That when He comes He'll say 'It is enow*
> *Unto itself—'twere better let it be:*
> *It is so small and full*
> *And has no need of Me.'*

9 | Stewards of the Planet

We are all too easily awed by the very size of the universe as it is depicted by modern astronomy. Science cowes us, even bludgeons us, with mathematical data — the vast distances, the billions of galaxies, the infinite aeons of time through which this huge lifeless mechanism of gaseous and electronic vortices has been turning. How unimportant is the life of man on his tiny planet, we are told — a flare of a match struck momentarily in the vast darkness, burning itself out after a transient and ephemeral instant of consciousness. And we are asked to believe that this mechanistic structure of the universe is all that exists, all there is to reality. The terrible and autocratic authority of science silences the protests of imagination and even of common sense.

In the early 16th Century, the mechanistic image of the cosmos evolved by Copernicus demonstrated that the earth was not the center of the solar system, but that it revolved around the sun like the other planets. During the ensuing centuries, proliferating rationalism reduced the universe to mathematical formulae, human life to mere chance and natural selection, man to a mere observer, a helpless bystander. To study the cosmos, man, as Ernst Lehrs says, has made himself into a "one-eyed color-blind pointer reader." He has developed the detached consciousness of an onlooker, whose very intellectual apparatus alienates him from the nature he contemplates. Instead of being a part of an all-encompassing whole, man has become an outsider, a pariah in his environment.

The Copernican Revolution reduced man to a status of no significance in a vast and dead mechanism, a chance accident of evolution. And by ironic paradox, this very demotion of man from his central position led him to an unprecedented arrogance, a monstrous presumption that allows him to exploit and pollute the planet to his own advantage, with no regard to the consequences. If man is of no significance in a world that is wholly indifferent to him, why should he not do what he likes for his gain or pleasure? Cooperation, participation and respect give way to a mentality of dog-eat-dog, a grim and ruthless battle for survival at all costs.

Now, however, basic human instinct, vision and the new spiritual science are rising in protest. To quote John Cowper Powys in his essay on Walt Whitman:

> *Surely such a limited universe is a grotesque and preposterous substitute for the teeming Reservoirs, Levels, Regions and Dimensions of Life, which not only the mysticism of Walt Whitman, but the natural normal inevitable mysticism of ordinary humanity, the mysticism that springs from the calmest and clearest portion of the human mind, feels assured must be discoverable, somehow or other, in the bosom of the All.*

The pre-Copernican system, as propounded by Ptolemy in the 3rd Century A.D., posited the earth as the center of the solar system, around which the planets, sun and moon moved and poured their effluences. Beyond was the sphere of the fixed stars and, beyond that again, the Heavenly Spheres of the Empyrean and the "Primum Mobile." As for the planets, they were conceived of as "crystal spheres," and the orbit of each was believed to mark the boundary of its field of influence. Earth was seen to reside at the center of the planets' movements, and the effects of Mars or Saturn, for example, could thus play directly upon the human being. Man was thus always *in* all the planets, and they in man. Man, as the great experiment of

God, was in the center of the cosmos. The true science of astrology rests on this same geocentric perspective.

Laplace, Napoleon's astronomer, supposedly declared: "I have searched the heavens with my telescope and I have found no sign of God." But the mistake is to assume that Copernican astronomy explains all that is, and that there can be nothing more. The Copernican system effectively describes how the mechanism of the solar system works, but that is all it does. To treat it as anything more comprehensive is like describing the technical arrangements in a theater, and forgetting that the real purpose of the edifice is to convey the energy, wisdom and power of a play. Ultimately, Copernican astronomy shows us no more of the total picture than a garden path shows us of the curve of the globe. We may certainly accept it as an explanation of the movements of the heavenly bodies. At the same time, we *can also* accept that reality is a more complex matter, and that — on a different and more spiritual level — earth *is* the center it was once deemed to be. The mathematical formulae and calculations do not preclude higher worlds of beings, which cannot be apprehended by the ordinary senses or intellect. To create bridges into such spheres, we must intensify our thinking, and the beings of the higher worlds must lower their vibratory rates to meet us in new dimensions of consciousness.

To neutralize our sense of awe when faced with astronomical figures, Teilhard stresses that it is not size that matters so much as molecular complexity. The vast "red giants" among the stars have an exceedingly simple molecular structure. On the other hand, the temperate planet earth has achieved such "complexification" that self-consciousness has been raised to an unprecedented degree in the fabulously complex brain and body. Thus our earth, tiny in size, can carry an infinitely precious cargo. In consequence of this, it has been held worthy of divine attention. And this in turn suggests the infinite importance of man in the cosmic scheme, and explains the present concern for his welfare apparently felt in the higher spheres. For man has now reached that point in evolution at which he can allow awareness to expand, and so achieve cosmic and God-consciousness. We are entering the space age not only with our rockets, but through the expansion of mind, to meet the intelligences of the universe.

The spiritual view of the universe, then, restores man to a plane of central importance. This, by contrast, brings to us a new and true humility — quite different from the arrogance bred by materialism and its mechanistic perspective. If we are integrally part of the whole of living nature, we are indeed stewards of the planet, given "dominion over the fish of the sea and over the fowl of the air and over every living thing that moveth upon the earth." What have we done with our stewardship? The answer is appalling. But we can yet make good the terrible damage we have inflicted on the living earth and its creatures — damage for which, through our greed, we are directly responsible.

The dynamic and spiritual view of the universe now opening to our understanding does not in any way belittle the great intellectual accomplishments of modern astronomy. It complements that view while at the same time offering a broader and more meaningful context — and one that transcends the pessimism of rational intellectual humanists like Bertrand Russell:

> *That man is the product of causes which had no prevision of the end they were achieving; that his origin, his growth, his hopes and fears, his loves and his beliefs are but the outcome of accidental collocations of atoms; that no fire, no heroism, no intensity of thought and feeling can preserve an individual life beyond the grave; that all the labor of the ages, all the devotion, all the inspiration, all the noonday brightness of human genius, are destined to extinction in the vast death of the solar system, and that the whole temple of man's achievement must inevitably be buried*

beneath the debris of a universe in ruins — all these things, if not quite beyond dispute, are yet so nearly certain, that no philosophy which rejects them can hope to stand. Only within the scaffolding of these truths, only on the firm foundation of unyielding despair, can the soul's habitation henceforth be safely built.

Now we are beginning to awaken to a brighter alternative — the new certainty that, seen from a different perspective, the Ptolemaic system still reflects a certain profound truth. Whatever its physical mechanics, the universe can still be teeming with spiritual energies and qualities of being. Life on earth can be a part of the life of the entire universe. Distance is irrelevant. We experience that consciousness can be anywhere instantly. As Andrew Glazewski says, "Our consciousness is not in our body: our body is in our consciousness." At will, consciousness can be anywhere in its vast field, the body merely being the focal point for its operation in earthly life. Our "ego" is where we choose to direct our attention; it can instantly be where it sends its thought. And when we remember that thought can move faster than light, the vast distances of modern astronomy cease to appall or intimidate. The spiritual world view thus restores optimism and opens a new dimension of vision.

The possibilities inherent in such a view are admirably summarized by John Charles Earle's sonnet, "Bodily Extension":

The body is not bounded by its skin;
Its effluence, like a gentle cloud of scent,
Is wide into the air diffused and blent
With elements unseen, its way doth win
To ether frontiers, where take origin
Far subtler systems, nobler regions meant
To be the area and the instrument
Of operations ever to begin
Anew and never end. Thus every man
Wears as his robe the garment of the sky —

So close his union with the cosmic plan,
So perfectly he pierces low and high —
Reaching as far in space as creature can,
And co-existing with immensity.

10 | The Polluted Planet and the Living Spirit

A BRIEF LOOK around us compels us to admit that "Spaceship Earth" is in a bad way; and it is we men who have upset the balance. It seemed to us once that the resources available to us were infinite and inexhaustible. Now, to our chagrin, we are discovering that we are consuming "capital" at an alarming rate. We are using up the world, and polluting it into the bargain. Aware of this ominous prospect, some of us feel that we have seen the "writing on the wall."

The purely materialistic view of life is obliged increasingly to acknowledge apparently insurmountable problems. In contrast to that position stands the spiritual world view. This view entails a universe shot through and suffused with living Creative Intelligence and Being. Creative Spirit is recognized as the origin and source of all things, and from it the phenomenal world is derived. We come to discern the reality of a great Oneness of Absolute Being, which has divided its unity into subordinate hierarchical levels. These provide the archetypal ideas from which material forms have been poured into manifestation. "In the beginning was the Word . . ." Until recently, people have tacitly assumed that matter was the primary reality and that the universe was a dead mechanism. Now our collective consciousness is being flooded with an alternative realization — that spirit is primary and that the great Oneness interpenetrates the temporal world in all its diversity.

This basic hypothesis can obviously be applied to any aspect of life. Let us now apply it to the great threat of our age, pollution. Our first witness will be the astronaut Edgar Mitchell. In the following passage, he describes his first glimpse of earth after orbiting behind the moon:

There have been few of us privileged to experience the mystical and soul-rending feeling of floating through endless space and looking back to see home, the beautiful jewel of earth. After months and years of perfecting the testing of an immense system of man and machine which would place me there in space — all of that was but a foreshadowing of my realization of the place man has in the scheme of the universe. We are part of a universe of consciousness. I sensed this out in space. I devote my life to the discovery of what this means for me and for all humankind.

We, too, more simply but no less validly, can explore space, simply by reaching up in imaginative meditation. In inner stillness, the consciousness is lifted above the atmosphere of earth. We move up, into the velvet darkness of the sky beneath the "majestical roof fretted with golden fire," and, floating in orbit beyond the pull of gravity, look down upon the turning earth in its beauty. It is not difficult to feel its organic life, to see it as a creature of the cosmos, an organism imbued with sentience, to conceive of it as a living Whole, capable of inhaling and exhaling the life forces and energies of space, with a bloodstream of magnetic and etheric currents and points of power and light like glands, or chakras, in its surface. Every cell has its core of energy and spirit, while the whole earth has its consciousness and is full of vital energy. Yet in that layer of highly evolved consciousness which surrounds it, that "center which we call the race of men," evolution has become conscious of itself. Mind in man responds to mind in the universe and yearns for union with it. We men, integrally part of our mother earth, are her faculty of thought. And mankind has reached that stage in its development that allows consciousness to be expanded, enabling thought to blend with the higher intelligences. This is what, in our small way, we are approaching in meditation and creative imagining. Indeed, it is unlikely that we can imagine anything which does not on some level already exist as a precipitation of divine imagining.

Thus, as a mental exercise, we *can* create a higher plane. In our tenuous subtle body, we can walk a landscape of equally tenuous substance, but one that is also beautiful and filled with light. Through meditation, we can move in those regions the soul visits in sleep, and in which it sojourns after death. Space is filled with myriad levels of being and consciousness, all interpenetrating. "In My Father's house are many mansions . . ." To conceive reality in this imaginative way instills in us a vision of earth as an organism within ever greater organisms, and the whole alive. Everything is ultimately spirit, in different conditions of density. Space exploration in our age need not only be by rocket; it can also be through lifted consciousness across the frequency bands.

From the perspective of a spiritual being, let us look down upon Earth. What is going wrong? Why is it so dark? Why can the higher worlds no longer make contact? In part because man, through his intellectual development during the last few centuries, has cut himself off from the whole to which he truly belongs. He has lost all knowledge, all recollection, of the reality of higher worlds and of the hierarchy of planes of being. He has lost both spirit and God. To the supernal spiritual perspective, therefore, the world appears dark and silent. Intellectual, self-conscious, self-sufficient man has misplaced all sense of his real purpose in it. Cut off from his spiritual source, satisfied with the brilliance of his investigations into physical nature, he becomes a denier of the spirit and believes the universe to be a vast dead mechanism. Conceiving himself to be a chance accident in evolution, he feels entitled, for his own advantage and greater glory, to exploit what he deems to be the dead mineral body of the planet. An ungrateful and spoiled child, he has lost all recollection that this is his mother earth, his true mother, an ensouled creature, and that he is part of it, as a blood corpuscle is integrally part of an organism. Failing to apprehend the miracle of interrelatedness in the complex balance of all nature, he rapes the earth in his ignorance, arrogance and greed.

Looking down from a spiritual dimension, we can experience and appreciate the marvellous harmony of earth life. We can discern the incredible complexity of the pattern and how, in all its diversity, it is a working unity, delicately poised in its constant movement. It has been said that Earth is a planet of wisdom, and that it is the task of man to transform it, during the coming epoch, into a planet of love. But when we compare the chaos of our emotional life with the beauty of the working of natural law, we must confess that we have yet a long way to go. We can see how man is integrally part of the oneness of nature, yet we watch him acting as if he were an outcast alien in a nature wholly indifferent to him — not realizing that he himself is responsible for that indifference. We watch him polluting air and water and soil and recklessly planning to release radiations which he will never manage to control, yet which he knows may do irreparable damage.

From our hypothetical vantage point — that of a spiritual being among other such beings — we know by direct vision that the harmony of the complex life pattern on earth is not an isolated phenomenon, but part of the life structure of energies in the cosmos. The solar system, the whole universe, all that can be conceived, is a spiritual organism. From distant galaxies, energies can be released which are instinct with intelligence and with love. We can therefore appreciate that a man-made catastrophe on earth would be retrograde to all cosmic life and evolution. We know that man is a great experiment of the divine world, a project or blueprint for developing a spiritual being able to sustain the responsibility of free will and evolve into both co-creator and friend of God. We also witness the culmination of an epoch, with the step into widened consciousness looming ever more imminent. And we watch with anxiety lest, so near his goal, man destroys himself, unable to transcend his egotistical greed. Nevertheless, scattered groups and individuals are beginning to recognize their true spiritual nature and strive towards union with their higher selves. As this occurs, and as the cry for help and contact with spirit rises upwards, the darkened planet begins again to glow in points and centers devoted to meditation and communion with higher realities. Through such centers, the power of the living spirit can be earthed. Their light constitutes an invocation to the redemptive forces of Light.

The High Intelligences of the universe are working for the harmony of all life, and will not tolerate the condition of an errant Earth fraught with discord, hatred and negative emotion. Thus there is a readiness to make contact with man wherever and whenever he shows himself open and sufficiently awake. And, if we can accept the evidence for continuing consciousness and individuality after so-called death, the picture becomes brighter still. Our friends and colleagues, who, while on earth, were concerned with the issues of planetary conservation, will still be capable of throwing their weight into the rescue operation. Their effect, through a telepathic influence on our own thinking, must not be discounted. The work continues from both planes, and the whole movement is not weakened, but strengthened when some influential figure moves on to operate from a level of widened consciousness.

In confronting the problems of pollution, we must never lose sight of earth's place as a *living* organism in a *living* cosmos. It is from this implicit foundation that the new science of ecology endeavors to explore the intricate balance and interrelationship of all life. For the first time, intellectual understanding is beginning to grasp how the planet's organism works as one in all its complex diversity. And ecology drives home all the more emphatically the appalling things we are doing to the world we inhabit. There is no need to describe them here in any detail. It is sufficient to read Rattray Taylor's *The Doomsday Book*. As a leading ecologist, Taylor shows, in terms we can all appreciate and understand, how easily the delicate balance of life and atmosphere can be disturbed, if not disastrously disrupted. He explains, for instance, how we might well bring down upon ourselves a "heat death" which would turn temperate Europe into an arid desert — if we do not first bring down a new ice-age. Either is easily possible, he warns, and within the life span of our children. The terrifying prospects he evokes make his book read like a horror story. But it is not fiction.

Ecologists know that our salvation lies in learning how to THINK WHOLENESS. This, however, is something we are not yet trained to do. Technology is quite incapable of it, the sense of wholeness being utterly contrary to its intrinsic character. If a new invention can be launched, it must go ahead, whatever the cost. If a new machine can fly faster, fly it must. Economics cannot think wholeness. And for our culture, the test of worth is economic — whether or not something pays. As long as profit remains a primary value, the mind cannot turn to wholeness. Besides, we have lived at least two centuries of intellectual rationalism, and have got so imbued with the experience of separation from the spirit that the very concept of "the One" is an alien, even laughable, metaphysic.

How, then, do we learn to think into wholeness? What constitutes the qualifications for doing so? The answer lies with those who have achieved initiation into higher knowledge, whose intuition has been so developed that — as seers and sensitives — they can blend thinking with the world processes and thereby expand consciousness to become one with the realms of spirit. What we are talking about is a totally new form of human mental activity, which can speak directly from the whole. It does not discourse *about* the spirit, but, through direct experience, issues *from* the spirit. This higher knowledge therefore provides a genuine touchstone as to what we may or may not legitimately do to the living planet. At the time of the first high-altitude nuclear tests, certain sensitives in this country cabled the President of the United States. They warned him that, by rending the etheric envelope of the atmosphere, we would grant access not only to dangerous radiations, but to dark and evil principles which would attack the very soul of man. Predictably enough, their advice was disregarded. Had it been accepted, we should have witnessed the kind of cooperation that is now even more necessary — cooperation between leading ecologists on the one hand and, on the other, those who can supplement scientific knowledge with spiritual wisdom. This would provide a gauge of how far we can afford to go in our treatment of the living earth. And meditation, too, can be an important adjunct to science if our planet is to be saved.

We have endeavored to conceive of the earth as a sentient being, a living organism. We have seen what man, in quest of profit, has done to it. He has polluted the rivers, lakes and seas, filled the air with noxious fumes, recklessly destroyed the tree cover, poisoned the soil and — by his blind use of chemical fertilizers and pesticides — damaged the life cycle of the plant world. It would hardly be surprising if the living earth were to strike back in retribution! How long will this great being tolerate rape and desecration by the primary repository of intelligence on her surface? Man, who was entrusted the task of stewardship, has instead demonstrated only his greed and ignorance. To quote one paragraph from Dr. Schumacher's important book, *Small is Beautiful:*

> *The continuation of scientific advance in the direction of ever increasing violence, culminating in nuclear fission and moving on to nuclear fusion, is a prospect of terror threatening the abolition of man. Yet it is not written in the stars that this must be the direction. There is also a life-giving and life-enhancing possibility,*

the conscious exploration and cultivation of all relatively non-violent, harmonious organic methods of co-operating with that enormous, wonderful, incomprehensible system of God-given nature, of which we are a part and which we certainly have not made ourselves.

We are violating the living body of the earth to which we belong, and she is writhing under our abuses. But earth is also part of a cosmos of living pulsating energies imbued with life. The whole is a great spiritual organism. We men are not each an isolated mind, but each a pulse of the universal mind experiencing the illusion of separation. Here is the factor we ignore in all our thinking. Communications from higher intelligences warn us that we will never solve our problems if we continue to think of the earth as an isolated unit in a huge dead mechanism of the universe. It is, rather, an integral and important facet of the greater pattern of consciousness, and there are energies now being released which can redeem the pollution we have produced. It is likely that we have gone so far in our evil and ignorant ways that repentance — the Greek word is "metanoia," which means "change of thinking" — cannot in itself repair the damage. We need, in other words, the aid of higher power. That power *does* exist and *is* alert to the crisis. In this fact lies our hope.

We cannot afford to ignore it. Roberto Vacca's book, *The Coming Dark Age*, warns of the appalling catastrophes that loom ahead, that are indeed inevitable if present trends continue unchecked. Nevertheless, we can aspire to the coming of a new age that will avert disaster. It may be a "near run thing," as Wellington said of Waterloo. The Creative Intelligence perhaps revels in games of brinksmanship. But there is still time, if only just enough — provided we can learn collaboration with the energies of light. We must conceive of them pouring invisibly over and around and through us. They are backed by the vitality of the creative source. They are alive and intelligent and filled with love. They can sweep away obstacles like a river in flood. When accepted by the instrument designed for their operation — namely the human being — they will bring vision and creative power.

The old society and the old methods are patently losing vitality. Eventually, they may simply run down, deteriorate and wither away. As this occurs, the new will manifest, precipitated into form by universal impulses working for harmony. There is ample energy to satisfy human needs, energy connected with the spiritual sun and therefore not fraught with the desperate dangers of nuclear power. Granted, we are in the throes of an energy crisis, but it contains a new, vital and as yet largely unacknowledged factor. New sources of fuel, conducive to our collective salvation, are working in close affinity with the Creative Intelligence of the universe. If we attempt to use these resources for greed, financial profit or war, the Creative Intelligence might well withdraw its influence and decline to cooperate. The result would be far greater chaos than that which surrounds us now.

For many rational minds, the possibility that must be confronted is a strange one. We may simply be compelled to admit that spiritual forces and beings are involved, and are a reality. If and when the prophesied changes begin, it may well prove necessary to explain to a frightened and bewildered public exactly what is happening. Television may prove to be a vehicle for something more important than facile entertainment; political and governmental authority may have to acknowledge the reality of beneficent spiritual powers from outside the planet. In consequence, a profound revolution in thinking could rapidly come about, once events begin to occur which cannot be explained away rationally. For we must remember that living ideas are continually penetrating our minds and breaking down old barriers of resistance, preconception and prejudice.

The prospect is not one of blind optimism which chooses to ignore contemporary trends and pretends that all is well. On the contrary, we must be fully cognizant of the appalling, even unthinkable, calamities which might overwhelm us if the present structure collapses. Yet we have a certain assurance — that though catastrophes descend, the influx of the transforming and vitalizing energies of the New Age will quickly follow. "Operation Earth" is perfectly timed, and all is already known. Our great hope lies in the principle of a "Higher Command," intent on the work of universal harmony. It recognizes the urgency. It recognizes that never before was there such a drama. Our epoch is indeed a living saga or myth in which we are all involved and have a unique role to play. So bleak are the present prospects that we *must* strive to "think wholeness," in order that the ignored and neglected factor may be understood, and our forgotten and invisible allies brought into full operation. "Look up, for your redemption draweth nigh."

Through man came pollution. Through man, therefore, must come redemption from pollution. Man is the bridge between the two worlds, material and spiritual. Since he is the point of self-consciousness in the body of earth, he must be the instrument to channel the cleansing power of the light. Since he has freedom of choice, it is for him to determine whether, where and when that power shall flow. A reorientation of attitude within man will open the floodgates. First, however, he must see and understand his position in the very soul of the cosmos. Then he must take on himself the task of invoking the high energies of the forces of light. There must be no false modesty, no diffidence arising from a sense of inadequacy. We must, with all due humility, accept the responsibility of calling on the Creative Intelligence, which is God. The initiative lies with man. Nor does it require any inordinate numbers. All that is necessary is a diffusion, a dissemination of living energy, which will instantly permeate the whole organism of earth, like an injection into the bloodstream. But there must, as at the fall of Sodom, be a *sufficient number* of dedicated groups and individuals.

We must elicit an impulse from the spiritual which can transmute and activate every cell. It is a power that can BE in the whole universe and, simultaneously, within the core of each atom. And it is this same power of the Logos which, in nuclear fission or fusion, we release in a downwards negative direction, a direction that leads to uncontrolled destruction. Now we must learn to tap it creatively, by lifting consciousness into its supernal field. Only then can that which is polluted be redeemed. In *The Form of the Fourth*, Mary Fullerson suggests that elevated thinking will enable the individual so to enter and accept the fire of the spirit that physical cells will be transformed and rendered immune to the pollution of their environment. We must cultivate techniques of cleansing and catharsis, thus preparing ourselves to receive the "ordeal by fire." It then follows that the requisite power, by divine dispensation, will enter the very heart of matter to transmute and cleanse polluted earth, air and water by molecular change.

At present, it is as if our world were suffused by an anti-life impulse, a diabolical influence using the human vehicle to undermine the harmonious unity of existence on earth. The chief manifestation of this infernal factor is greed and the insatiable passion for profit. And the infernal factor will perpetuate its dominion as long as the primary motive for action remains economic advantage. Such motivation constitutes a pollution of mind and character, corresponding to that of the earth itself. On every level, then, the satanic forces are joined in battle with the spirit.

All our pollution problems must be tackled positively. We must cease committing acts which threaten life. We must also include in our programme, as a perfectly realistic and practical process, *the channelling of love, light and spirit into the body of the Earth*. In this way, we will inaugurate a chain reaction of healing against which the forces of pollution, decay and death will be unable to stand. It is with this vision, and supported by this power, that we must take *our* stand against that which desecrates our world.

Organic husbandry has recognized that the soil is a complex

living organism, and that there is a cycle of life in plant growth — from seed through leaf and flower and back to humus and new seed. This cycle is interrupted and destroyed when artificial fertilizers are employed — quite apart from their propensity to decrease the soil's fertility. To understand all the implications involved, we must go further than the teachings of the Soil Association and recognize that elemental beings and nature spirits are indeed a reality. What our Celtic ancestors knew as "the little people" represent forces of living and creative intelligence working in the plant-world. Although they are non-corporeal beings, the "devas" are also the architects of plant design, and the nature spirits are the "craftsmen" working to fulfil the life cycle in individual plants. Modern clairvoyance is rediscovering the reality of the elemental world in nature, and there is increasing evidence that we can no longer afford to neglect its role.

Is it purely fanciful in these rationalistic times to speak again of the nature spirits? A single example may provide an answer to that question. At Findhorn, in Morayshire, a remarkable experiment in cooperation between man and the invisible worlds was undertaken — a New Age community in which all aspects of life were dedicated to serving the spirit and its purpose. At its inception in 1962, Peter Caddy, the founder and custodian of this now large and flourishing center, settled on a caravan site amid barren windswept sand dunes which could only grow spiky grass and pine trees. With him were his wife, a very remarkable sensitive, and a friend with developed faculties of clairaudience.

According to "guidance" they received, they were to start growing vegetables — an apparently absurd enterprise, given the inhospitable soil and their lack of gardening experience. Perplexed, they turned to the devas and requested aid. In response, Dorothy received, almost instantaneously, a clear telepathic message. Acting upon the advice given them, they proceeded to their task. In three years, a thriving garden of glorious flowers, magnificent vegetables and abundant broad-leaved trees and shrubs was growing. Now, the sandy waste is utterly transformed and the garden is a veritable enchanted world of outstanding beauty. The quality of vegetables and plants is unsurpassable. And there is no explanation as to how the "miracle" occurred, except the claim of cooperation with the nature spirits. Certainly no artificial fertilizers were employed. Soil experts with long experience of organic husbandry investigated and declared that compost alone, in such an environment and in so short a time, could not possibly have brought about the transformation. The phenomenon simply cannot be explained away.

The implications of the Findhorn experience are of profound importance. In one of the devic messages to the Findhorn community, it was stated that "one garden can save a world." The whole unified field of consciousness of the nature spirits knew at once that a group of men had made contact, and was willing to cooperate with them. A response was forthcoming, demonstrating that such cooperation can indeed turn the deserts into blossoming gardens and purify the pollution of the planet. A similar fantastic adventure is open to us, if we choose to avail ourselves of the opportunity. The first step clearly requires spiritual vision, united with science and practical skill. But the path is hardly inaccessible. On the contrary, it was indicated in Rudolf Steiner's Biodynamic system of horticulture and agriculture; and, more recently, research in America has provided scientific demonstration of an astonishing sensitivity in plants, hitherto inconceivable. All these developments are surveyed in *The Secret Life of Plants*, by Peter Tompkins and Christopher Bird.

There is something fabulous about our relation to the plant-world, as revealed by this new vision. It is as if a new realm of subtlety were opening before our eyes. It is becoming increasingly apparent that human thinking and emotion are integrally linked with the vegetable kingdom; and recent findings offer more and more testimony as to how crude our past dealings with nature have been. Once we believed we were battling to conquer nature. Now we are beginning to see that we are ourselves part of its delicate complex, intimately connected with all its domains.

To the "onlooker consciousness" of our intellectual age, man appeared a chance accident in a world of nature wholly indifferent to him. Now, with the discovery of the etheric field of vital forces working within every form as a complex unity, we find that we are a responsible factor in the working of the whole. On a more profound level, the entire sweep of evolution is reflected and experienced in us. This applies to our relations with the world of plants as well. We are now starting to see that the archetype of man was there from the beginning as a divine idea, and that it is reflected throughout the kingdoms of nature — as if every species were a specialized facet of the human organism. In one sense, we might indeed say that man has risen to his true manhood through the sacrifice of nature. From a larger and more spiritual perspective, however, it is obvious that we *are* nature and nature us.

We began this chapter with an imaginative picture of the earth from a viewpoint in the cosmos. Let us now return to that picture. Intuitive communications through friends in the beyond tell us that an etheric mantle of light is gathering around the earth from the finer and purer vibrations of the cosmos. "And I saw a new Heaven and a new Earth . . ." This field of subtle life-filled forces is to impregnate the whole earth, and the spirit of earth as a whole will rise to meet it. As that happens, human consciousness, an inseparable factor in the earth consciousness, will inevitably be lifted towards another dimension. Then there will be a blending in thought between those on both planes — embodied or disembodied — who are linked by the greater love. But we are warned repeatedly that there is no time to lose, since this extraordinary process is occurring now and the inconceivable blending of the timeless with time is already in process. In other words, the polluted world is being cleansed on the etheric level, and every man, in his freedom of choice, is invited to be a part of the event. Teilhard expresses this in his experience of the Mass on the World in "Hymn of the Universe":

> *It is done. Once again the Fire has penetrated the earth . . . the flame has lit up the whole world from within. All things individually and collectively are penetrated and flooded by it, from the inmost core of the tiniest atom to the mighty sweep of the most universal laws of being; so naturally has it flooded every element, every energy, every connecting link in the unity of our cosmos, that one might suppose the cosmos to have burst spontaneously into flame.*

Is this vision really just so much poetic fantasy? Is it nothing more than a mere "wild hope," in Teilhard's words, "that our earth is to be recast"?

We may answer that question with a brief summary of certain key points stressed in this chapter. To overcome pollution in all its aspects, the spiritual energies from the Cosmos must flow into the body of the Whole Earth, as well as into the bodies and souls of men. And man himself is the necessary link and instrument which will make all this possible. The redemptive flow has already begun, and its workings are apparent to those sufficiently developed to perceive it. Ultimately, nothing can stand against it.

11 | Apocalypse Now

OUR CULTURE IS obviously in a time of trouble. Many have foreseen breakdown in our economy, since a great technology obsessed with getting rich quickly is too clumsy and top-heavy, and altogether too inhuman in its values. Avarice leads to rivalry and competition, to the "law of the jungle," in other words, and this leads in turn to fear and conflict. In the meantime, ecologists are becoming aware of how delicately poised the living organism of the ecosphere is, and that our reckless exploitation of the earth's resources may well lead to retribution. And seers and adepts of the age, with their developed powers of intuition, foretell a great spiritual crisis or turning point for mankind by the end of the 20th Century. Twenty years remaining! Our present difficulties may well be the overture before the ringing up of the curtain for the grand opera. It is therefore necessary to see current events and complexities in a broader context, as component skeins of an enormous canvas. It is too sanguine, too naive, to assume we can just patch things up and carry on. We must learn that merely getting more possessions and satisfying more desires and supposed wants is not the object of life. We shall have to simplify our lives drastically and be prepared to let go much that we now strive desperately to hold. Values and consciousness must change, not just tastes, manners, fashions, social structures or politics.

Most attempts to solve our problems are made from within the context of narrow materialistic philosphy. In such attempts, therefore, a critical factor is neglected, a factor which offers the potential of the most supreme hope man has ever conceived. This is the emergence of the broad cosmic view which recognizes that we are all part of a living universe, shot through with creative spirit and made up of energies which permeate every part of it — energies imbued with intelligence and love. The earth must be seen as a living seed, rather than a fragment of dumb mineral in a vast mechanism of a dead universe. Higher intelligences do indeed exist, are very much concerned about the future of Planet Earth and may be contacted by human thinking. To put it another way, we may forget God, but He is not going to forget us.

We are now reaching the end of an age when, in the long evolution of consciousness, man can step beyond the limitations of ego-bound desire and expand his understanding. He can now achieve cosmic consciousness and blend with the breadth of spiritual being; but this cannot come about if he clings frantically to all his fancied material wants. Therefore, much must be jettisoned if the great next step is to occur. "Except ye repent, ye shall all likewise perish." As we have noted, the word "repent" did not originally carry the connotations of sin and guilt that it does today. It derives from the Greek word, "metanoia," which can be translated as "change of thinking." Our present anxieties and disasters will not be dispelled until we achieve such a fundamental change of attitude and values.

The cosmic energies now being released may well sweep away the negative aspects of materialism so powerful at present on earth. Out of catastrophe, a new society may be born, comprising all souls who can tune in to the New Age and give themselves wholeheartedly to its manifestation. Our age of anxiety, in short, is apocalyptic in its nature, and the coming of disasters will not be truly understood unless we see them as a prelude to spiritual awakening and redemption. It is clear to those with heightened intuition that if man chooses to go on treating the earth as an isolated unit in a dead cosmos, he will never resolve his difficulties. On the other hand, if he can awaken to the reality of the creative spirit in the universe, he can cooperate with higher intelligence and can bring a veritable new world into being. It is a fantastic prospect and a sublime hope at a time when potential cataclysm of his own making looms portentously before him.

Let us therefore look at the great symbolism of the Apocalypse. It pertains, of course, to a new advent, a new dispensation, seen in a great perspective of past and future — with, it would appear, our present age as the crucial turning point. Here, for example, are some verses from Matthew, Chapter 24:

Ye shall hear of wars and rumors of wars: see that ye be not troubled, for all these things must come to pass, but the end is not yet. For nation shall rise against nation and kingdom against kingdom, and there shall be famines and pestilence and earthquakes in divers places. And these are the beginning of sorrows. For then shall be great tribulation such as was not since the beginning of the world to this time, nor ever shall be.

Immediately after the tribulation of those days shall the sun be darkened and the moon shall not give her Light, and the stars shall fall from heaven and the powers of the heavens shall be shaken.

And then shall appear the sign of the Son of Man in Heaven, and then shall the tribes of the earth mourn and they shall see the Son of Man coming in the clouds of heaven with power and great glory. And he shall send his angels with a great sound of trumpets and they shall gather together his elect from the four winds . . .

Verily I say unto you, this generation shall not pass till all these things be fulfilled.

A great tribulation immediately followed by a supreme hope. And this may pertain directly to us. The words were written two thousand years ago, of course; people expected a Second Coming then, but the allegory may have been phrased to hold good for the moment when the great evolutionary change reached mankind. And this it seems may be now, as we move from the Piscean to the Aquarian Age, and the waters of the spirit are poured out into human consciousness. Thus the word "generation" may refer to the end of the zodiacal cycle.

According to what is called the Doctrine of the Avatars, man has never been utterly without hope. Whenever, in the entire course of its history, despairing mankind has united to send up an agonized cry for help, an Avatar or Saviour has appeared from the higher planes. Krishna, in the *Baghavad Gita*, says to Arjuna:

> *Whenever there is a withering of the Law and an uprising of lawlessness on all sides, then I manifest Myself. For the salvation of the righteous and the destruction of such as do evil, I come to birth age after age.*

May it not be that what we are now witnessing is the advent of such a savior on the invisible planes? The power of cosmic love — not just our personal emotional love, but the experience of the great Oneness of all Being within all life — could flood through human consciousness, inevitably breaking down and sweeping away that which resisted it. It will come as a pressure into our lives, lifting, searing, cleansing and perforce appearing at first as an angel of death and destruction to that which works in accordance with the negative laws of avarice, selfishness or violence. The coming is a phenomenon, an event which, by its impact, will first throw men into confusion and distress. For those whose understanding is open, however, the chaos and turmoil will be followed by a flood of unbelievable joy, a new and exultant courage, as heart and mind surrender to the fire of the new and exalted influx.

This age could be ours, now. It could literally be true that "this generation shall not pass away till these things are fulfilled." As Teilhard has stressed, man has now reached that point in evolution when ego aggrandizement begins to give way to the greater goal of widening consciousness, which leads soul after soul to "home upon the Omega point." Through expanded awareness, scientific intellect could now take a leap into true knowledge of the Spirit. Indira Gandhi, in a speech at Ottawa, pleaded for a "breakthrough of the mind":

> *The marvel of the living mind is that when it is illumined it can move into uncharted territories. It is enabled to take this step not out of reaction to the hurts of the past, but through the miracle of liberation from them.*

And the late Tudor Pole wrote:

> *It is my belief that the 'Revealer of the Word' (the Christos) for the historic times in which we live, has already descended into the invisible spheres that surround our planet and that those with eyes to see and ears to hear can begin to discern the message He is bringing, even though the Messenger may not be clothed in form or outwardly discernible.*

And Teilhard says, in a passage we have also quoted before but which is worth citing again:

> *. . . the wild hope that our earth will be recast . . . At all costs, we must renew in ourselves the desire and the hope for the great Coming . . . What is the cause of this disorder in society, this uneasy agitation, these swelling waves, these whirling and mingling currents and these turbulent and formidable new impulses? Mankind is visibly passing through a crisis of growth. It sees the universe growing luminous like the horizon just before sunrise. It has a sense of premonition and expectation . . .*

The star for which the world is waiting is, necessarily, Christ Himself, in whom we hope.

The veils which hide the invisible planes of spirit are now exceedingly thin. A new spirit can come in glory in "the clouds," meaning the etheric plane which becomes visible to us as our vision expands. Thus, the outpouring of its impulse could sweep through human consciousness, firing heart and mind and will. For those who understand, it offers a prospect of exultant joy. For those still fettered to the lower self, however, it may appear an outpouring of the Vials of Wrath, sweeping away all that works according to the old laws of self-aggrandizement and avarice. It is for this reason that T.S. Eliot speaks of "Christ the Tiger." In *Little Gidding*, he says:

> *Who then devised the torment? Love.*
> *Love is the unfamiliar Name*
> *Behind the hands that wove*
> *The intolerable shirt of flame*
> *Which human power cannot remove.*

But "wrath," like "repent," derives from the Greek; and if we check its original meaning, we find that the word once meant "an impassioned movement of the soul." That definition is extremely illuminating. It invests the force of Biblical "wrath" with quite different associations from those we usually attach to it, and signifies something very different from a God of Vengeance. It is only when men resist the approach of the "Hound of Heaven" that the vehemence of spiritual love seems to resemble anger.

No doubt the whole apocalyptic picture we have drawn sounds a bit melodramatic, a bit sensational. We must remember, however, that we live in sensational times — times that would seem a lurid nightmare to people living a century ago. "Affairs now are soul size." Our problems, in short, have assumed positively planetary proportions; and to resolve them, we must adapt our imaginative thinking to the widest possible canvas. There is no question that things look grim when perceived from the standpoint of materialism. And even to the visionary eye, the terrible abuses man has perpetrated on the earth seem to warrant retribution. But let us suppose that the truth inherent in the Apocalypse is an allegorical one. Let us suppose a new advent is really imminent and the floodgates of love are opening. That supposition is a factor wholly ignored in most analyses of current events. And that very supposition offers a supreme hope in this age of apprehension and distress — a hope which can fire man with a new ardor and creative power. The breakdown may indeed be a prelude to a new dawn. And since the alternatives are so unmitigatedly bleak, it is surely worth betting our bottom dollar on the grand possibility. Mankind channelling energies from higher intelligence in the universe can redeem our polluted planet. The spirit of the cosmos, visible and invisible, can be brought to birth within each human heart. Here burns the "wild hope."

We are all involved personally in the world's suffering and potential redemption. "These are but the beginnings of troubles." But — "look up — for your redemption draweth nigh." It is not comfortable to live in an apocalyptic age, but, if one's understanding is in focus, it is certainly exciting. And it is an immense privilege to be involved. All that is now happening can be seen as a trial, an ordeal to be experienced and overcome. Events must be perceived on their true scale. To quote Christopher Fry:

> *The human heart can go to the lengths of God.*
> *Dark and cold we may be, but this*
> *Is no winter now. The frozen misery*
> *Of centuries breaks, cracks, begins to move;*
> *The thunder is the thunder of the floes,*
> *The thaw, the flood, the upstart Spring.*

Thank God our time is now when wrong
Comes up to face us everywhere,
Never to leave us till we take
The longest stride of soul men ever took.
Affairs are now soul size.
The enterprise
Is exploration into God.
Where are you making for? It takes
So many thousand years to wake,
But will you wake for pity's sake?

A new society is being formed by those souls who *do* wake and open their hearts to the reality of the spirit and of its power. Its abundance will provide enough to satisfy the needs of those whose hearts are centered upon it. Not the wants or desires, but the *needs*. We may be certain that, as outward conditions worsen, our invisible guides will draw closer and show themselves the more ready, even eager, to help. And this factor is of profound importance. Telepathic contact is open to us from a plane lifted above the present confusion. We must therefore wake up, look up. We can learn increasingly to live in the present moment, confident that we shall be shown the next step and that we shall be led safely through unprecedented and difficult circumstances. The opposing forces of darkness may work their evil — as the rising tide of crime and violence indeed attests. But the worse things appear to be, the more we must fervently embrace the hope of the light which will follow. There can be an extraordinary phenomenon, a flooding of love through human hearts which would link with all others who have seen the great vision. The "Great Coming" can lift people into joy and creative action.

In no previous time of change, throughout all recorded history, has man been so strongly supported by such high power. The New Age is not someone's imposed plan, not a system devised by the rational intellect, but a recognition that cosmic

energies imbued with higher intelligence and with love *do* exist
on the invisible planes, waiting to sweep through human consciousness. The wind of the spirit is blowing. Babylon, with
all its wastefulness, deception and extravagance, may fall, but:

> *I saw a new heaven and a new earth . . . and I heard a great*
> *voice from the throne saying: Behold the tabernacle of God is with*
> *man and he will dwell with them . . . and God shall wipe away*
> *all tears from their eyes and death shall be no more . . . Behold,*
> *I make all things new.*

That astonishing document, the Book of Revelation, seems
to speak directly to our present condition. In Chapter 12, for
example, it describes how the dragon, the Beast, is thrown down
to earth:

> *And there was war in heaven: Michael and his angels fought*
> *against the dragon; the dragon fought and his angels. And pre-*
> *vailed not . . . and the great dragon was cast out into the earth . . .*
> *having great wrath because he knoweth that he hath but a short*
> *time.*

This implies that the battle for the light has already been won
on the higher planes, a fact confirmed by communications received from the high spiritual sources. The ultimate victory
for goodness is assured, but what transpires on earth during
the interim depends on human endeavor and understanding.
Armageddon is indeed being fought out within human hearts,
and outward events merely mirror the condition of the soul.
Inner and outer worlds reflect each other, and what occurs to us
we have brought down upon our own heads. Again, however,
we must *look up*. The energies and intelligence which can and
will redeem mankind are indeed imminent. All men are being
called into their service, for without human initiative and invocation, those energies cannot be earthed. We must provide

the bridgeheads for the coming invasion—or, more properly, for the coming liberation. And we must acknowledge that it will not be as easy as we might like it to be. The forces of evil are obviously rampant and fighting back desperately. And we must recognize that we are indeed facing dark and sinister impulses of evil, demonic principles thirsting for power, both overtly and behind the scenes. Hence the urgency of acknowledging the reality of invisible and light-giving forces, for any naive denial of their existence opens the door to dark possession of the soul and will. A single glance at our surroundings is sufficient to convince us that the devil is having a field day —precisely because, in our materialism, we do not recognize his existence. Rudolf Steiner distinguishes two malevolent principles at work in our world. Mephistopheles, Ahriman, the Lord of Darkness, is the denier of the Spirit, dragging consciousness down into the morass of materialism. Lucifer, or Satan, is the tempter who draws man into inflated egoism and lust for power. Both of these forces—sometimes covertly, sometimes with astonishing and brazen openness—ravage our world, infecting everything, presiding over all that conduces to pollution, both of our inner and outer environments. And these forces can only be held at bay by the power of light, love and spirit in the heart. If we take no cognizance of the principles —good and evil—at work around us, we are indeed in peril. But a guarantee of protection lies in invocation of the forces of light. Thus, the Apocalypse is indeed relevant to our understanding of the evils of our time, and to how we may overcome them.

It is worth taking a second example to illustrate this point. In its closing chapters, the Book of Revelation depicts the Fall of Babylon and the descent of the Heavenly Jerusalem. At the same time, those two cities are identified with two women, "the Whore" and "the Bride." It is important that the Book does not refer to the whore *of* Babylon. Rather, the city *is* the woman; the woman symbolizes a whole culture, a whole hierarchy of values. The fall of Babylon, then, represents a sweeping away of the soul qualities and attributes associated with the greed and self-seeking of materialism.

The images of the Apocalypse imply and portend a great cleansing of that within our culture which allows selfish exploitation of the earth's resources, as well as repression of truth in the name of profit-making. In his greed, man has polluted the planet and failed in his stewardship. Now he calls down evil on himself, for the evil is so rife that cleansing by some greater power has become necessary. Without the aid of such power, we alone cannot hope to redeem the situation. But if a great spiritual impulse were to surge through our society, it would bring catharsis of mind and heart. It would undermine the greed which causes so much fear and cruelty, and would attack the debasing materialism of our age. It would mean the advent of a united human movement for harmony, goodwill and cooperation. It would mean a great awakening to the service of the earth as a living being. The immense hope lies in seeing present events as the beginning of a transformation in mankind, which will entail a purgation and exorcism of social dross and evil — even if the cost is suffering and distress in individual lives.

Using these principles to illuminate the text, we may turn again to the Book of Revelation, specifically to Chapter 18. There we find Babylon described as:

> . . . *a great city that was clothed in fine linen and scarlet and decked with gold and precious stones and pearls. And when they saw the smoke of her burning they cried, 'What city is like unto this great city?'*

The Whore Babylon represents all that constitutes greed, desire and the "lusts of the flesh" in an age of materialistic values. She is described as the woman . . .

arrayed in purple and scarlet color and decked with gold and precious stones, having a golden cup in her hand full of abominations . . . upon her forehead was a name written MYSTERY, BABYLON THE GREAT, THE MOTHER OF HARLOTS AND ABOMINATIONS OF THE EARTH.

As a prostitute barters herself for money, materialistic culture has bartered itself — itself, its true nature and its participation in the divine worlds. But now:

Babylon the Great is fallen, is fallen, and is become the habitation of devils and of every foul spirit. Alas, alas, that great City Babylon, that mighty city, for in one hour is thy judgment come.

Jerusalem, in contrast, is described as a "Bride adorned for her husband," and, with Babylon's fall, the Heavenly City descends. It has always been present, of course, on the ethereal plane, but now it must be realized on earth. It is to be formed out of every particle of matter and every human soul that can be imbued with the power and light of the spirit. This is the cosmic "take-over bid." And whereas Babylon was established from the below upwards, Jerusalem descends from above. The long story of the Fall of Man has, at the same time, been the story of the spirit's materialization. The coming reascent of man entails the spiritualization of matter.

In Chapter 20 of the Book of Revelation, we find the following passage:

Come and I will show thee the bride, the wife of the Lamb. And he took me up in spirit to a great high mountain and showed me the holy city Jerusalem coming down out of heaven from God, having the Glory of God. And the light there was like to a precious stone, even as crystal . . . And the building of the wall thereof was of jasper stone; but the city itself pure gold, like to clear glass. And the foundations of the wall of the city were adorned with all

manner of precious stone . . . And the city hath no need of the
sun nor of the moon to shine in it, for the glory of God hath
enlightened it.

The city's gold, of course, symbolizes the power of the sun,
while the precious stones represent the influence of the stars.
The gates of the city are described as pearl — another powerful
symbol, for pearl is a substance created by transmutation of
pain into beauty. It is through these gates that we shall enter
the city. Inside, the divine light of the cosmos unites with earth.
From there, the darkened planet can begin to shine with divine
radiance.

Babylon, then, is to be thrown down into the abyss and the
beast to be "chained a thousand years." That which works
according to the old laws of avarice must be overthrown to
give place to a New Age. It is obvious enough that the impetus
behind many things in our present economic structure is de-
pleted, on the verge of collapse. The wheels of materialism
may soon cease to turn. But the New Age has behind it the
infinite reservoirs of cosmic energy and power. Man, dedicated
to cooperation with higher intelligence in the service of the
spirit, begins to work with a strength that is unlimited. As we
have said, much must fall away, and we must certainly recognize that a species of cleavage will manifest itself in human
kind. But it would be a mistake to see this as a distinction
between the élite and the lost, between sheep and goats. Those
awake to the spiritual realities behind present events will be
lifted into direct contact with the Christ, their hearts and minds
filled with the joy and ardor of the advent. Those who have
rejected it are not lost, but will, after the great changes, be
gathered on a different vibratory rate or plane. They, too, will
be shepherded, and receive in time a new opportunity.

12 | Christ and the Adversary Forces

We have spoken of the powers of darkness. We have noted that evil is a very real phenomenon and that it seems to be rampant in our age. We have said that the devil is having a field day. But what do we mean by these terms? Who or what precisely is the devil?

From his research into the invisible worlds, Rudolf Steiner established a distinction between two demonic forces which constitute a polarity and exercise the greatest adverse influences on the evolving soul of man. It is important to note that we are dealing with a duality, for — if we think of him at all — we tend to think of the devil as a single being. We must distinguish, however, between Lucifer, the fallen angel, the Light Bearer, the Tempter, and Mephistopheles or Ahriman, Lord of Darkness, the denier of the spirit, the eternal negative. Lucifer and the beings and influences who work for him are responsible for that trend in the soul which inflates man's egoism, which kindles his lust for power. The fall of man as myth reflects the descent into the material world. We go through the age-long ordeal of expulsion from the Innocence of Eden Garden, to use Blake's phrase, and pass — by becoming enmeshed in matter — into Experience. It is from this Experience that, in time, we shall be released by achieving Imagination, the entry into the New Jerusalem.

The "expulsion from Eden," the adventure of descent into the gravity plane of earth, involves man's experience of aloneness and separation. Man evolves to self-consciousness. He discovers he has free will. This is the gift, the great challenge, responsibility and opportunity. Man is invited to develop into a being who can reflect God, and so become His companion. The angels do not enjoy free will in this sense. Their joy and purpose and nature is to serve that of which they are an intrinsic part. Man alone is that order of spiritual being which enjoys the possibility of free creative activity. And for this very reason, Lucifer has the opportunity of tempting him. Under Lucifer's influence, man seeks not to become one with God, but to *be* God, to usurp the divine throne and occupy it himself. Lucifer plays upon the nascent ego and inflates self-consciousness to the point of narcissistic intoxication. Man creates not for God's greater glory, but for his own; he revels in himself and his ideas, investing himself wholly in intellectual pride. The result is a monstrous, swollen egoism.

The Renaissance and the centuries following witness that phase in the evolution of consciousness during which the self-conscious ego strives to increase its power. The close identification with the body and its five senses leads man to loss of contact with his spiritual origin — to forget the reality of higher worlds and to delight in his own power and enjoyment of the material. The Luciferic impulse works in the soul to titillate the sense of freedom for the ego. Thus Lucifer, the Light Bearer, can draw a man away from his true path of finding the light in his heart. The Light Bearer offers a false light, which tempts man even while he pursues spiritual knowledge.

The complementary influence to Lucifer is Mephistopheles. He is the same diabolical force which the Zoroastrian wisdom of ancient Persia called Ahriman, the Lord of Darkness, who opposed Ahura Mazdao, God of Light. In *Paradise Lost*, Milton concerns himself primarily with Lucifer. In *Faust*, Goethe's attention is devoted to Ahriman/Mephistopheles.

Ahriman drags the human soul ever deeper into matter and the world of the senses, thereby denying the reality of the spirit.

He is the eternal negative. In Goethe's *Faust*, as we have seen, he describes himself as the principle which always negates and denies: "Ich bin der Geist der stets verneint." We see Ahriman working in those trends of thought which regard the universe as a dead mechanism. He is the power behind materialism. He is often the voice of cold and clinical cynicism, of mocking laughter, of icy insensitivity — of what many people mean, in short, when they speak of "being realistic."

Under the Nazi regime, Germany was dominated by Lucifer. Our modern culture, in contrast, owes its chief impetus to Ahriman. We are an Ahrimanic civilization, lacking virtually all awareness of the reality of higher worlds of spirit. It is Ahriman who tempts us to deny the divine origin of the soul of man. And his influence is all-pervasive. It operates in modern science, which focuses man's attention on the dead workings of matter; in astronomy, whose calculations repudiate the vision of the cosmos as shot through with living intelligence and creative spirit; in our financial systems, which reduce value to crude numerals in dollars or sterling; in medicine, which sees man only as a physical body hardly different from a machine; in psychology when it ignores the higher self in man and presumes to "heal" the ephemeral personality; in much of modern agriculture, which diminishes the earth to a lifeless repository of exploitable resources. The price that modern man has paid for the development of his acute intellectual faculties and his self-consciousness is the atrophying of the organs of perception, which enabled our ancestors to be aware of the spiritual worlds.

Thus we come eventually to deny our divine origin. Some people today even speak of the "death of God," because they can no longer find Him. They fail to recognize, of course, that the loss of the divine is equally explicable by the atrophy of our organs of perception. When those dormant faculties are reawakened, however, we can rediscover that we are part of an immense living whole and that Mind is everywhere.

Thus the intellectual faculty which makes our great scientific and technological civilization possible is developed at the cost of spiritual awareness. We have de-spiritualized the world precisely to the extent that we have humanized it. And, denying the existence of spiritual beings as so much old superstition, we are left at the mercy of Ahriman and his minions. Unrecognized, they can work unhindered in human thought, dragging us ever deeper into the morass of the material. Until we recognize their reality, we obviously have no power to oppose these principles of evil. There is a profound truth in the tradition that, if we can call the devil by his name, we can overcome him. Too often, we simply do not discern that evil entities can possess our souls and drag us down into darkness. Herein lies the importance of the churches' renewed interest in exorcism. Many disturbed souls *are* in fact suffering from possession, either by dark entities or by other earth-bound souls. Without the knowledge and techniques for dealing with such contingencies, psychology is at a loss and Ahriman will have his way.

Man is the great experiment of God. By developing towards freedom, however, he runs the risk of losing all touch with the divine will and the spiritual worlds. Materialism in itself is not necessarily evil. On the contrary, it has been the great spiritual task of Western man to explore and master matter. Teilhard de Chardin, for example, has inspired us to awaken to the holiness and beauty of matter as the receptacle for spirit. But much materialistic thinking involves the narrowing of the focus of our vision, with the consequent danger that man completely loses sight of his spiritual origin. Then he may fall into a new bestiality, the more terrible for being conscious. He may be caught in a debased or depraved sensuality, or manifest a personal self-aggrandizing egoism. Ahriman and Lucifer tear the soul in two directions and away from its true course of evolution.

What we call "evil" occurs when these two demonic impulses get out of control and begin to run amok. In their elemental nature, they need not be evil. On the contrary, they are necessary. Their task is to be the tempters, without which the human soul could not experience the education earth has to offer. We must not complain against the "referees" who arrange the hazards in our obstacle race. We must accept those obstacles as something to be surmounted, knowing that "to him that overcometh shall be given the crown." In some sense, therefore, Lucifer's rebellious deed can be seen as a sacrifice, in order that man be allowed the requisite tests and trials. In time, Lucifer will himself be redeemed. So, too, will Ahriman. When either gets out of hand, however, when either is allowed to destroy our sense of perspective and blind us to the broader context, "evil" is the result.

How, then, is true balance to be attained, true perspective to be established and sustained? It is obvious that we *must* work with Ahriman, since he is the force which controls the material world in which we live. And, at the same time, we must also develop idealistic vision and activity of the ego, which are Lucifer's province. The purely practical man, devoid of vision, will be lost, while the idealist must have his feet firmly planted on the ground. Luciferic aspiration must filter down into the Ahrimanic regions of a technological culture, but mystical vision must also remain anchored to earthly reality.

True balance is achieved through the presence of the divine impulse in the heart. Steiner expressed this truth in a great sculptural grouping, thirty feet high, which he carved in wood to stand in his great center for spiritual science in Dornach, Switzerland. He called this the "Representative of Humanity." With a majestic gesture, Christ holds Lucifer in control, a winged figure in the air above Him. At the same time, by the power radiating through His other hand, Ahriman is contained, a Mephistophelian figure lurking among the roots of the trees in the field of gravity. In this sculpture is the image of threefold man redeemed. Man is a being of thinking, feeling and will. As in all life, the unity is maintained through the balanced working of the trinity of systems. But until man has awakened the spiritual impulse within his heart, he is in danger. One or the other of the two demonic forces will perpetually strive to ensnare his soul and hurl it into confusion and imbalance.

It is particularly urgent in our age of spiritual awakening to recognize the polarity of negative forces, held in balance by the positive power of light—the Christ. It is clear that, as we approach the great spiritual turning point in the closing years of this century, the veils between the two worlds will grow thin, and spiritual energies will be released. Though neutral in themselves, these energies can be "hi-jacked," as it were, appropriated and usurped in thought and will by Lucifer or Ahriman. And we oppose them in blindness until we recognize their reality.

Steiner foretold that Ahriman would actually incarnate in a physical body, as Christ did two thousand years ago. He need not manifest as a political or flagrantly materialistic leader, of course. On the contrary, he might appear as an occultist, for example, a splendid and beautiful young man who could lead successive generations of mankind astray. The wiles of Mephistopheles are infinite, devious and ingeniously labyrinthine in their workings. But they do continue to work, as a dark and living force.

Needless to say, the same applies to Lucifer. In such apocalyptic passages as Matthew 24 and Luke 17, we are admonished against the deceivers:

> *Then if any man shall say unto you: here is Christ, or there, believe him not. For there shall arise false Christs and false prophets and shall show great signs and wonders, insomuch that, if it were possible, they shall deceive the very elect.*

They have already appeared. They are doing so at present and will continue to do so, with greater and greater frequency and impact. And we cannot afford to minimize their potential influence. Lucifer can divert a genuine spiritual impulse within a soul or a movement into a patent perversion of the light. By the vulnerability of his own egoism, man can be deceived into betraying his true task. Even unconsciously, a spiritual leader can become an instrument of Lucifer. It is more frightening still when such voluntary submission to possession is conscious and deliberate. We have already had to contend with one such instance in our time. In *The Spear of Destiny*, Trevor Ravenscroft chronicles how Hitler placed himself at Lucifer's disposal, and how the entire pantheon of Nazi leaders employed techniques of dark occultism and black magic in their quest for world power and racial domination.

Among those involved in any spiritual movement, there is always risk of Luciferic infiltration, through the channels of egoism and self-aggrandizement. The Antichrist may work through the vehicle of ostensible light. We must be perpetually on guard, for in the near future new movements may well arise, outwardly plausible, which are nevertheless the instruments of the demonic. The present revival of interest in black magic is symptomatic. Through naive fascination with the mysterious and forbidden, unwitting souls may be snared and led astray, abdicating their spiritual birthright for sheer power or sensuality. Through drugs, black magic rituals and other fashionable shortcuts to spiritual or psychic experience, the soul's development may be seriously retarded, if not arrested.

We live in a time of spiritual awakening. Mankind is reaching the stage in evolution when a great step forward can be taken towards cosmic consciousness. A new age is indeed dawning. It should hardly be surprising, then, that forces which deny and distort spiritual knowledge are struggling ever more furiously to establish their dominion. The Battle of Armageddon has been truly joined. Each soul is the battlefield, and each must choose his affiliation, pledge his allegiance. Tolkien's great myth of the conflict of the Light and Darkness is powerfully relevant to our epoch.

If we do not recognize Lucifer and Ahriman, we are always vulnerable, always liable to be led astray. These principles can play upon our innocence, and twist or exaggerate our positive qualities into instruments of evil. It is obvious enough that without spirit, man can become a heartless creature. Powerful intellect and remorseless will can channel a lust for power, as our era has abundantly witnessed. And the danger is not by any means past. The dark forces function on all planes of being, and the soul which places itself at their disposal will continue to exert an influence beyond the grave. Nazism did not die with Adolf Hitler. And if Lucifer suffered a temporary setback with the fall of the Third Reich, it is now Ahriman who stands triumphant.

We must therefore ask ourselves how we are to counter the demonic wiles. They are highly intelligent and sophisticated, these workers for darkness, and will attack at the most unexpected moments. If protection against them is to be maintained, we must learn to be continually alert, prepared at all moments of the day to call for spiritual help in our defense.

As a means of protection and a key to the humanity of the New Age, we must remember Steiner's image of the Christ holding the redeemed Lucifer and controlled Ahriman in creative balance. We must remember the simple but great principle that the dark forces give way before the light of the Christ. In meditation and in moments of crisis, we can direct our thought to the light, can call down the shaft of light to suffuse our thinking, heart and will. In our creative imagination, we can surround ourselves with a cloak or protective sphere of radiance. The descending beam of light can be received in the heart. There it will be transformed into love for all being and so directed outwards again to meet and transmute the encroaching darkness. A powerful meditational symbol is a cross of light surrounded by a circle or sphere — the Iona cross of Celtic Christianity seen three-dimensionally — with the heart-altar at the crossing where the star can shine. This great archetypal symbol is a wonderful image for the Grail.

The rays of love can be directed towards the eternal being within each soul or form. However evil a man may be, he can be redeemed by light and love, a force which no evil can ultimately withstand. This has been confirmed by accounts of underground churches behind the Iron Curtain. In numerous instances, it has been demonstrated that evil can be disarmed. If a man can regard his torturer with love, recognizing an imperishable divine core within a deluded soul, the adversary will be rendered helpless. In this connection, it is worth reading *Tortured for Christ*, by Wurmbrand. This book reveals what is happening today in the martyred churches of Eastern Europe. Their predicament echoes that of the early Christians sacrificed in the Colosseum. Those martyrs were undefeatable; knowing the presence of the Christ and their own immortality of soul, they went through torture and death with joy. The same virtue is apparent in their successors of our epoch, which so parallels the decline of Imperial Rome.

We would do well to embrace these contemporary martyrs as examples. They are a beacon for us, and their suffering underlines the immense gravity of the present situation — the dangers posed to man's soul by the ruthless workings of Lucifer and Ahriman. At the same time, their unswerving tenacity epitomizes the awakening of the all-conquering Christ within the human heart. For Michael and his angels do battle with the dragon . . .

13 | Meditation—
The Gateway

MEDITATION HAS BECOME so vital a factor in new age activity that it warrants some attention in itself. This chapter, therefore, offers an elementary answer for those who inquire about what it is. We will make no attempt to present a comprehensive survey of the various methods. We will offer, rather, a simple approach, accessible to anyone in its initial stages.

Essentially, meditation is the technique of creating a center of quietude and stillness within the self and then allowing this center to be flooded with light from the higher planes. It is the route to inner contact with the realms of eternal being. In our hurried and anxious world, where everything is rushed and frantic, it is not easy to be inwardly still. Thoughts, emotions and the concerns of the day crowd into our minds and fill any potential vacuum of quiet. They constitute an incessant distraction. It is therefore all the more precious if we can achieve a spell in which we are quite freed from the incursions of active thoughts. This chapter offers a practical basic approach to attaining such freedom.

First, we must withdraw to some place which is itself still. Ideally, we should have a sanctum in our house where complete privacy is possible, but any quiet place will suffice. We must sit comfortably so that we are as unaware as possible of our bodies. The spine should be vertical, so that power can flow through us from high sources, but, in the beginning, forgetting of the physical body is most important. The East, of course, uses the 'lotus position,' feet folded and crossed. For many people in the West, however, this is difficult and uncomfortable, and is quite unnecessary for our initial approach. It is sufficient to be restfully seated, hands lightly folded in the lap or placed on the knees. We must then close our eyes and sit in absolute physical stillness. While maintaining our upright sitting position, without slumping, we must release all unnecessary tension, relaxing forehead, eyes, jaw, neck, shoulders and so down through the body and limbs. As far as feeling is concerned, everything in us should be still — except the breathing. And we should be aware of this perpetual gentle rhythm. We must turn our attention to the breathing and attempt to watch it — in : out : in : out. Tibetan practitioners watch the air being inhaled and exhaled through the nostrils; the Siamese insist that we be mindful of the gentle rise and fall of the solar plexus. Mindfulness of breathing is a basic exercise. Various schools of Buddhism use it as a training in directed thought, and aspiring adepts are taught to master it through long hours of meditation. For our initial steps in the West, however, such ambitious objectives are superfluous. We should simply be concerned with creating the center of stillness and for this the mindfulness of the breathing rhythm is most helpful, running like a thread through our period of meditation. At the outset, it is desirable to take perhaps three slow deep breaths, exhaling steadily and fully. This helps to change the rhythm of thinking and still the self. Then, as we watch the breathing happening on its own, we shall probably find it growing ever more gentle. With this shift, our mood will also become still, until, in deep meditation, we really cease to be aware of any breathing at all.

At some point, roving thoughts may enter our minds and distract us. In imagination we may see ourselves enter a chapel, close the door and seat ourselves. It may be a circular chapel with a dome, a symbol for the individual, who will experience his inner self as a hollow space. Suddenly, like an intruding bat or bird, a stray disturbing thought may wing its way into the chapel. If we offer it no lodgement, however, no point on which to alight, it will fly out again, leaving us in peace. Thoughts only become operative when we acknowledge them and accept them. In the outer world, we must naturally deal with them as they assail us. We must grasp them and respond to them, employing whatever act of will may be necessary. But in the silence of our inner chapel, for this precious half hour of inner peace, they have no place. We need not actively oppose them, or mobilize our will as a defense. We need only withhold any response to them and watch them fade like smoke passing through the window. "Stilling my thinking, I inhale . . . and exhale . . ." Watching the breathing — not *doing* the breathing — provides us with a positive alternative to the unwanted thought, without any strenuous self-conscious attempt to force the mind into emptiness. And soon, a great stillness will begin to permeate our consciousness. The chapel will become completely silent.

A quality of stillness will rise through feet and limbs and pervade the body. We may even feel it like a tingling in feet and legs. We must give the body over to the earth. We may even sense dimly that it is truly a part of earth, a tiny focal point in the body of earth, where this great being has become heightened in consciousness. We must hand body back to earth and let it melt into stillness.

In meditation, we do not so much think stillness as experience stillness. "Experiencing the stillness, I inhale . . . and exhale." Then, from stillness, we will shift subtly to the experience of tranquility. This is associated less with the body than with the heart and emotions. It is a soul experience, counterpart to the bodily stillness. One can feel heart melt into the plane of tranquility; one can feel the gentle rhythm of the breathing flowing through it, as if the heart itself were drawing in and giving out the life force.

At last, we will experience the profound state of peace, which penetrates the head, the thinking. This differs both from stillness of body and tranquility of heart, but is another facet of the total meditational experience. Stillness — tranquility — peace — : a trinity of kindred states which include body, heart and mind. The physical functioning and the nervous system are brought into a condition of complete rest, as in deep sleep, while the mind remains at alert attention. A rather remarkable accomplishment amid the world of busy thought and action and anxiety — personally, through our own directed thought, to create something that was not there before, a sphere or vacuum of stillness. So long as we maintain it, we can hold the clamorous world at bay.

So important is the attainment of this stage of inner quietude that it may appear almost an end in itself. For this chosen period in our busy day, we have found how to withdraw from the world and keep its impositions at a distance — by moving inwards and creating a chamber of silence in the heart. And the longer we can sustain our serene disengagement from mundane preoccupations, the greater will be our joy. Indeed, it can approach what is called "bliss consciousness," for it leads the soul towards that world of absolute being which exists as pure life and consciousness behind all manifestation in the relative world of things and events.

But this state is nevertheless but a step along the way. From it, we can begin to open ourselves to the higher planes of light. To be impregnated by the divine light from above is the second great objective, to which the first was only a means. Perhaps we should stress again that by "higher planes" we do not mean distance of vertical direction, for we are moving out of the world of space and time. We must rather recognize that the planes of being and extended spiritual consciousness are spheres of higher frequency or wavelength. There is light of the spirit behind physical light, a spiritual sun behind the physical sun. This spiritual light will fill the vacuum created by the individual who has achieved the inner stillness. Thus we may very gently allow light to flood through the dome of the chapel — in other words, the top of the head — and feel its way down into the heart until our whole being is suffused with it. At that point, we shall feel something happen in the heart. The imagination may take different forms. We may see a great shaft of light descending from the zenith and passing through our whole body, down into the earth — as if spirit were being "earthed." The sense of this power's descent may be quite strong, quite palpable; it will be intensified by our sitting position and vertical spine. The light will have entered through the "center" at the top of the head and been transformed in the heart center. It is as if the heart were a transformer and were giving out the light as love for all life. We can experience the horizontal outflow from the quiescent heart. It need not be directed at anyone or anything in particular. It is the beginning of the experience of the heart center as an organ, pouring out love for all beings. And, at this point, we will have realized in ourselves the symbol of the cross. As the breathing becomes ever more gentle, we shall have the beautiful experience that the heart center itself is breathing light. The body is forgotten and we become a species of vortex point for radiating the light of the spirit. The experience can be particularly significant and powerful when a group is working together.

The inner chamber, then, will now be brimming with light and silence. We can, if we wish, permit ourselves the experience of rising — as if, in a balloon lighter than air, we were passing up through the dark clouds. As we rise, the clouds become thinner and more translucent, until we break through into clear sunshine with the endless dome of the blue ether above us. The symbolism is obvious, for we are moving up through the emotional atmosphere of earth life to float clearly in orbit beyond the gravity drag of earthly concerns. Then we may bask in the radiance of the spiritual sunlight which penetrates every pore of body and soul. In this state, we may find wonderful peace. We may also begin to experience an expansion of consciousness, as if we were no longer tightly held by the limitations of the body. There is a profound mystery latent here—the fact that we look inwards in order to expand on a higher plane. But we are not indulging in rational, self-conscious introspection, analyzing our thoughts or motives. On the contrary, we are developing inner faculties which open onto widening vistas. Let us once again quote Blake's words:

> *I cease not from my great task—to open the Eternal Worlds, to open the Immortal Eye of man inwards into the Realms of Thought, into Eternity, ever expanding in the Bosom of God, the Human Imagination.*

Through meditation, we begin to understand that imagination is a faculty of profound significance, leading us towards contact with the divine worlds. It is certainly not the mere spurious weaving of fantasies. Our materialistic civilization is largely concerned with looking outwards. Meditation balances this tendency by turning us inwards and so through into realms of extended awareness. It is in the condition of absolute inner stillness and lifted consciousness that we can listen with alert attention and suspended thought for the speaking of the "still small voice." And we become simply an organ for listening.

Though the basic exercise is stilling the self and opening to the light, much may develop out of the state of inner tranquility and alert attention. We are truly becoming focal points for reflecting the higher worlds of thought. This may be apparent in imaginative pictures, and there is indeed a place in meditation for allowing the creative imagining to work.

Let us briefly develop one such image. We have set ourselves in a chamber or sphere of light into which the disturbing influence of the world has no access. Here, we lift above the murky psychic atmosphere of earth into the clear light of the spiritual sun. We receive the great shaft of light from the zenith, allowing it to pass down into the earth, and in the heart we transmute its rays to radiate out in the four directions of the compass, as love for all being. In this form, we may recognize that we have created the Celtic cross, but in three-dimensional form. It may well be experienced as an archetypal symbol for the New Age. At first, our own heart is the crossing point where light radiates as love. But the form can be enlarged indefinitely. Let it do so in the imagination until it stands like a great spherical temple with the altar and the six-pointed star shining in the center. This temple can be thronged with beings of light; and from this great spiritual lighthouse, we can beam out rays to link with other such centers. We can also direct the beams of light and love into the dark trouble spots of the world. Here they will provide the substance which spiritual forces can use to penetrate the fog of psychic darkness which, quite objectively, lie over such areas as Northern Ireland. Our image has a very real power, and we must accept that imagination is a creative deed. By meditation, we make an offering to the spiritual beings who can continue to use the great cross after we ourselves have withdrawn back into our mundane existence. As a group imagination, our power in this respect can be augmented. Such images can be allowed to form and they do indeed have their role to play in the affairs of our tormented planet.

In the beginning, however, our primary concern will be, as we have said, to create a still and listening center within ourselves. And eventually the time will come for return to our daily routine. Gently, we will fall back into the body, carrying in our heart the fine glowing light and warmth of the spiritual sun. During our meditation, we were open, on a soul level, to the light and its power. For that very reason, we should not plunge impetuously back into the earth vibration. The descent should be gradual, and one technique for ensuring this is called "sealing the centers with light." There are, as we know, psychic and spiritual centers in the brow, throat, heart and solar plexus; in imagination, we have "opened" the crown of the head. These apertures should be closed and protected by mentally placing over them the cross and the circle of light. It is also useful to visualize ourselves wrapped around in a protective cloak of light. Then we can safely move down again to meet the exigencies of the world, but carrying within us the inner stillness of the heart filled with light and love. That stillness will color and condition our responses to the outer world.

Half an hour is a good length for a meditation. If possible, it should be performed twice a day. Regularity in time and place is important, since it imposes a discipline and habit. Although many practitioners favor early morning, each individual is free to work out his own schedule and routine. Even fifteen minutes, however, is better than nothing; and a period of inner silence and stillness before entering sleep is of particular importance, since in sleep the soul establishes contact with the beings of the spiritual plane.

The need for meditation in our time cannot be overemphasized. If man's consciousness is to evolve and expand, more and more people must seek the silence and penetrate the barriers between the different levels of being. Meditation is a valid and safe way of doing so. It is therefore particularly desirable to embark on a meditative path. On the personal level, withdrawing into inner peace is not a selfish deed, but a necessary training. And through meditation, moreover, we become better members of the community. Tensions relax, and the love we experience within us is subsequently directed out into our surroundings. We also become more capable, more contented, more joyful and more peaceful — and something of all these qualities can be contagious, transmitted to those with whom we work in the world. There are other advantages to be reaped as well. Some people, for example, find that meditation improves their health. Others develop the capacity to receive guidance and help.

The methods and techniques of meditation vary a great deal, but all must include the inner stilling and the opening of the centers to the influx of light. The description we have offered is hardly definitive; it is simply designed to provide a general idea of the process. It also serves to demonstrate how meditation differs from prayer, although the two practices are obviously complementary.

In passing, we should briefly mention Transcendental Meditation, brought to the West by the Maharishi. Although based on Oriental wisdom, this form of the practice is particularly suited to the active modern Western consciousness. The Maharishi contends that the mind in itself has the capacity of flowing to the greatest source of happiness. This is the bliss of contact with the world of being or Creative Intelligence, which underlies our plane of time and space, the relative world. There is no need to force the mind into such contact. It is a question rather of finding the method by means of which it will most effectively gravitate towards this source of happiness. For this purpose, Transcendental Meditation adopts the use of a mantra, or sound, selected as suitable for each individual. Any thought or image could be used, of course, but the advantage of the mantra is that, being sheer sound, it has no immediate intellectual content, no associations or connotations. At the same time, it is not *merely a random sound*. On the contrary, it is a sound which is part of the primal language of nature, the primal nature of language, chosen from the ancient knowledge of the Upanishads. Inherent in any such sound is the capacity to home upon its creative source. When we pronounce it silently, it will therefore lead the mind away from the surface of our busy concerns, deeper and deeper inwards towards the realm of Creative Intelligence. At the same time, the nervous system is stilled and rested as in deep sleep. Needless to say, such rest is of inestimable value in our hurried and worried lives. And it provides the initial ground for all further and deeper experience.

We should also mention briefly the technique, developed, among others, by Reverend Robert Coulson, of Christian Contemplation. In this method, one of the 'I AM' phrases issued by Our

Lord is used as an object for silent contemplation, much like a mantra. In the silence, one may pronounce some such sentence as: "I AM the Light," "I AM with you always," "MY PEACE I give." Such sentences, spoken silently in the mind until they impregnate the stilled consciousness, eventually become the voice of the Lord Himself speaking to us.

Given the increasing interest in meditation, it is not surprising that many people should be turning to the teachings of the East, where the technique originated. At the same time, we should note that the emergence of spiritual science in the West has produced highly significant teachings on meditation which are particularly consonant with the intellectual development of our time. These uniquely Western teachings also pertain directly to Christianity. Their basic premise is that, in opening our centers to the spiritual light, they prepare us for the influx of the divine. By opening head and heart to the light, access is granted to healing powers for the ultimate redemption of mankind. And this principle relates to all humanity, regardless of creed and color. Through different methods of meditation, the wisdom of East and West may meet, for all religions offer facets of the truth of the Great Oneness.

14 | Man Attuned—The Hope for the Future

IT IS EASY to dismiss all we have said as so much airy idealism. What is its relevance, one might ask, in a world full of discord and dismay? As realists preoccupied with the population explosion, rising crime rates, violence, world famine and inflation, have we time for escapism into high-sounding ideas about the spirit? Perhaps this very understandable attitude is itself a form of escapism, a shuttering of our vision lest we be confronted with truths too tremendous, too intensely piercing to face. The fact is that many people fear the spirit. In it, they sense a power which can transform lives and burn away the dross of egoism to which they cling. And they shrink from the refining fire. Nevertheless, we are beginning to awaken to the extraordinary living forces permeating our lives and, according to our nature, we either accept it with joy and excitement or flee from its implications.

In either case, the effect is immediate and empirical. For as we said in our first chapter, we are not talking about some vague spiritual metaphysics, but the reality of living spirit working from the invisible planes, which can break through into our temporal sphere and transform human lives. The Great Oneness calls all its errant parts to blend and harmonize again within the pattern of the whole. Human self-will has drawn us away, and the confusion of our time demonstrates where separation has led us. To cooperate voluntarily with the transforming impulse is the great hope and challenge for man's future. The free and dedicated consciousness of evolved mankind is the instrument through which a new society and a new world is to be formed, for God needs man as much as man needs God. It is a new heaven as well as a new earth that is coming to birth.

Through meditation in the broadest sense, we can help establish the bridgehead. Though he is but a tiny unit in himself, man meditating is performing a deed of cosmic significance. We have imaginatively seen that each is a fragment of an immense whole. We are each responsible for releasing either jets of doubt and despondency into the body of earth, or for allowing an influx of light and courage. Since, as channels and conductors, we are endowed with free will, the light simply cannot penetrate unless we allow it to do so. Our awakening and our invocation make its entry possible. By each meditation, we align with a universal process. We have performed a willed deed which holds back the clamor of the world and creates a vortex point of stillness through which harmony and love can descend. Man is the catalyst that can allow the redemptive event to occur, so that the spirit can impregnate the body of earth. The transformation of man begins in ourselves and no one is too small or unimportant. The thinking of the heart is the field of action for the Higher Self. The whole reclaims the particle and re-unites it in attunement with itself.

Change man and you change society. Try to change society without the inner change in man, and confusion will be the sole result. And each conscious individual is solely responsible for making changes in himself. One basic spiritual law is that for each step into higher knowledge, a man should take three steps in development of his own character. This, when correctly implemented, protects against dark occultism that seeks personal power.

Lovingness, the power of spirit, can never stagnate. The heart, lighted by love, will radiate outwards, and the light will unite with itself in others. With joy, recognition will ensue, and groups will form by the attraction of mutual affinity. There is no bond like that of spiritual understanding, for it unites people of every type and age. It is the real social solvent.

And so new groups form, dedicated to the service of the spirit. These seed groups, contacting each other, are the matrix of a new society into which the power and quality of the spirit can work down into every aspect of daily life. It is, as we have emphasized before, a *new* society forming within the heart of the old. Perhaps it is building the new Ark to carry us safely through the deluge!

LET LIGHT AND LOVE AND POWER RESTORE THE PLAN ON EARTH

The groups we have mentioned form from individual souls who have been touched by the divine power, and who, through their own inner initiative, have tuned into it and accepted it. And such groups are appearing in many and varied forms. There are many meditational and healing groups which, though small, are learning a task of immense significance. There are the youth communes, many of which very naturally turn back to a simplification of life by renewed proximity to the living soil. It is clear that, with the impending prospect of world famine, man must learn to feed himself by organic husbandry on his own plots of land. "Il faut cultiver nos jardins." This brings with it a way of life that revives personal creativity through the need to do and make all that is needed. *Living the Good Life*, a book by Scott Nearing which describes one of the first such ventures in America, is most important in this respect. It provides a model for the small group which opts out of the "rat-race" to reestablish a genuine contact with nature.

But the new society, of course, must be able to tackle much broader problems; it is by no means only a return to simple living on the land. It must be prepared to make use of all the advantages of modern invention and technology, all the aids to living offered by a contemporary urban society. What has gone wrong with our culture is not its technical ingenuity, but the fact that it rests on a foundation of self-aggrandizement, voracious possession and accumulation. In contrast, the new culture will be based on what we can give to the whole, not what we can take from it. The art and mystery of giving must be relearned on all levels. Then we shall discover that abundance is infinite and that there is indeed enough for all.

Certain larger centers are in fact demonstrating how the living spirit can sift down into every aspect of daily life. Such a center is Auroville, near Pondicherry, founded on the continuing inspiration of the great seer Aurobindo. Here, a new age city is being built and the new laws applied in all aspects of the economy, all patterns of social relationship. In our country, perhaps the most striking example of a new age community is Findhorn. Here, in the north of Scotland, is a center which demonstrates the creative possibilities of the new age. It offers an indication of the way the living spirit can work through a human group. We have already described in an earlier chapter how, in cooperation with the nature spirits and the beings of the elemental world, Peter Caddy, founder and custodian of Findhorn, transformed a barren waste of sand dunes into a wonderful garden. But Findhorn is far more than a garden. It is a rapidly growing community wholly dedicated to the service of the whole. The area, a one-time caravan site, is now a veritable village, whose healthful and beneficent influence will radiate out into the entire region — and indeed, much further. It is a creative experiment in group living in which every member of the community gives to the full of his talents, every department contributing to the harmony of the whole and all concerned primarily with realizing the spirit on Earth. In 1962, Findhorn began with Peter Caddy's family and a friend. Now the community numbers two hundred permanent members. And as it expands further, the direct daily guidance on which it was founded has been deliberately withdrawn, so that each may learn to rely on his own inner guidance by attunement to the Higher Self.

Findhorn now calls itself a University of Light. Every aspect of its work is a facet of its educational vision. It has demonstrated the truth that in the spirit is abundance. Where the human will is wholly given to the realization on earth of the divine and where the self is attuned to the unity of life, inner intuitional guidance begins to work. It is revealed that the spirit will always meet the needs of those who serve it. Where the egoism, doubt and desire of the lower self are truly surrendered, needs will be satisfied. What is called the Law of Manifestation is being demonstrated at Findhorn. It holds the key to an economic revolution. In a new age society, the attitude to money will change drastically. We will come to see it as a means by which spiritual energy is facilitated in its flow.

The task of the new age community and groups is to allow the spirit to flow freely and creatively. All the clutter of outdated habits, possessions and thoughts must go, and life be simplified enormously. Then, as Findhorn attests, every aspect of life takes on a creative and even artistic quality, for quality is spirit, spirit quality. In the garden at Findhorn, in the cooking and preparation of meals, in the gatherings in the Sanctuary, in the flow of human contacts between both members and visitors, in the crafts and performing arts and in the recreational activities — everywhere, the joy of service to the whole manifests itself in quality and high artistic standards. Where people with artistic gifts make a genuine breakthrough in consciousness into the higher planes, it is natural that they should express this breakthrough artistically. Sir Donald Tovey defined genius as "the most effective channel for the creative source." The spiritual world view surely offers the greatest inspiration for literature, painting, music, sculpture and all other arts. It is the eternal theme of Man seen vitally and freshly. We might almost prophesy a new renaissance, as more and more artists blend consciousness with the higher worlds of creative Ideas. There will then be new need and inspiration to express the vision in artistic symbolism. Living Ideas will play again through creative man in new forms of fresh expression.

This, too, is occurring at Findhorn. At the same time, there is also an increasing interest in a revival of the crafts. The conviction of the sacredness of all life and the divinity latent within all material intensifies the significance of craft work. Delight in the creation of quality through long and patient treatment of beautiful material can again become the motive, particularly when the work is undertaken on behalf of the whole in a dedicated community. The mentality involved is akin to that which obtained, for example, in the illuminated texts produced by medieval monastaries.

Eventually, all aspects of daily life tend to take on something of a sacramental quality. Ritual naturally revives, and new rituals are created to celebrate special occasions and to mark the festivals of the year. These are often filled with a note of joy so characteristic of new age activities. Direct intuitive inspiration opens the possibility of a new ritual form, burgeoning with significance. And it brings a new meaning into the old rituals as well, as described in Mary Fullerson's book about the Eucharist, *By a New and Living Way*.

Findhorn is a particularly interesting and challenging example of the vital working of the new age impulse. It is but one example. We cannot, of course, do justice here to the breadth of the movement in Britain, America and other parts of the world. But once we acknowledge that energies from the invisible planes are at work in human consciousness, we will recognize the astonishing scope and variety in their present manifestations. New enterprises are continually springing up, new groups and ventures coming to birth. There are schools of meditation, centers for healing by the new therapies, colleges for study in the great traditions, seed groups for workshop study of the economic and social problems in the light of spiritual knowledge, religious movements which allow the wind of the spirit to blow, and much more besides. No one has a monopoly of the truth, since the emerging picture is of such vast extent. There may be differences of interpretation, but no one in any way touched by this spiritual resurgence can doubt that something of immense significance is happening. It looks as if the activity of the spirit, working through human enterprise, is seeking to display itself in very diverse forms and characters, so that no human soul will remain untouched by the new vision and denied opportunity to respond. And as the various movements coalesce and learn to work together, a most powerful united front will be presented, through which a pattern for the future can emerge. In this light is the hope for man's future, and it is bright indeed.

It becomes brighter still if we remember that we are not alone. Among the most significant of new age ideas — one to which we have alluded many times in these pages — is that of the invisible guides who help direct our destiny. If this idea is indeed valid, it extends the utmost encouragement for living forwards into the unknowable new. Most of us have experienced events which appear to have been strangely and ingeniously planned, and which cannot, we feel, be explained away by coincidence. These events can be ascribed to our spiritual guides, and, if we admit their existence in our own lives, we must acknowledge it in everyone else's. If a pattern reveals itself in small happenings, there must be a great web of direction influencing all lives, and national evolution as well. Once we learn to live into this idea, it will afford immense inner strength, and enable us to overcome the bugbear of doubt. Our inner evolution, as indicated by the Grail Knights in Wolfram von Eschenbach's *Parzival*, is to move from "Dullness" into "Doubt" and, from there, to "Security of Soul" or "Steadfastness of Thought." "Dullness" implies the crudely sensual life devoted solely to physical satisfaction. "Doubt" is the stage to which most of us have evolved. "Saelde"— security or blessedness of soul, is the stage we shall attain as the thinking lifts to contact the life of the Higher Self. This is the true Grail Quest for our time.

Civilization, in the true sense of that word, is now at a low ebb, but the possibilities of transformation are greater than ever before as the New Age dawns and the new energies flow. The signs are manifest in the new groups and centers we have described. The great revolution— and revelation— of our time is the reality of the living oneness of Being, now breaking through into our time-ridden lives. Evil, a very real force, is but the negative aspect of these energies. Once we grasp this, we can look up with joyful expectancy as we await the changes that even now are sweeping through our world.

The New Age centers are all parts of a great pattern. Research into lost knowledge now discloses how our forebears were sensitive to those points on the surface of the earth where magnetic power and spiritual light were especially active. They constitute vortices through which the etheric forces can impregnate the earth. Sensitives have found that, on these points, meditation and prayer are particularly effective, and contact with the higher worlds is particularly blessed. On such sites, therefore, temples and churches were established, to both signify and guard them. The sanctuaries and sacred groves of the Greek and Roman world indicated similar points of attunement with the invisible planes.

With the heightening of faculties of perception and the palpable thinning of the veils between planes of being, these ancient centers are being rediscovered and reactivated. Not infrequently, new age groups or ventures are unconsciously drawn to such sacred points and establish themselves there. Some sites have generated the closest modern approximation to medieval pilgrimages. We must visualize, then, a veritable network of light linking the groups who are dedicated to the service of the spirit. It may be likened to a great grid system on an etheric level. When the moment arrives for the throwing of the metaphorical cosmic master switch, a power of light and love will flood through this grid, forging it into a puissant vehicle for the revelation and manifestation of the spirit. And the pattern, of course, is worldwide.

The island of Britain appears to have been particularly favored with light and power centers. The great temples like Stonehenge, it now seems, were once centers for the earthing of the light. St. Columba was assuredly guided to the Holy Island of Iona, and so too were the followers of St. Cuthbert to Durham and Lindisfarne. St. Michael's Mount is a great power center, linked with many other Michael shrines, wells, hills and churches.

Britain has now ceased to be an imperial power. Standing between the mighty forces of America and the Soviet Union, she may now have a very special role to play in the spiritual awakening of mankind. Britain led the world in industrialization. Perhaps she must now take the lead in reversing the damage done by that process. And the inherent genius of the Anglo-Saxon race produced the political forms of democracy and contemporary social orders. Perhaps we must now assume the vanguard in shaping a new society, one in which the powers of the spirit can translate themselves into practical life. As in the pruning of a rose bush, limitation and loss may lead to flowering on another and more significant level.

The greatest and most perplexing truths concerning man's spiritual nature are enshrined in the symbolism of myth and legend. It is therefore appropriate, as this book draws to a close, to introduce a relevant allegory. Since so much of what we have said defies purely rational or intellectual proof, we must develop an intuitive understanding for what underlies the great fables and their expression in artistic form. Here, the most profound clues can often be found, which serve to enhance life's meaning and significance.

The ancient and colorful art of heraldry involved more than

the utilitarian function of distinguishing knights in the melée of a tournament. Like all symbols, the figures on heraldic coats-of-arms are repositories of truth and higher energy. On both individual and collective coats-of-arms, therefore, we may regard the two supporting figures — those holding the shield — as the relevant spiritual guides. Thus, the supporters of any people's arms can be seen to reveal something of the nature and spiritual task of a particular group-soul or folk-soul. On Britain's coat-of-arms, the two supporting figures are dexter, a lion rampant, crowned, and sinister, a unicorn. "Sinister," as in French, means the left side, the receptive feminine aspect preservative of life, as opposed to dexter, the active masculine aspect. Imperial Britain epitomized the crowned lion rampant. Now, however, the lion's day has passed. Now the unicorn is in the ascendant. The unicorn is a wonderful creature — a white horse with gazelle's feet and a shining horn on its brow. The horse traditionally symbolizes intelligence. The white horse, therefore, is purified intelligence, and the horn rising from the brow symbolizes the pineal gland, the third eye, the principle of enlightenment, illumination, initiation and higher knowledge of the spirit. And with its gazelle's feet, the unicorn can trip lightly over the morass of materialism. In legend, the unicorn is the familiar and attendant of a virgin, or priestess. She waits for it, submissively, outside a dark forest, from which the beast emerges to lay its head in her lap. Here, surely, is a magnificent symbol of the Higher Self, called from the realm of mystery to the fructification of the purified soul. If we look at Britain's unicorn, however, we notice that the animal's crown has fallen about its neck. Perhaps Britain's task is now to re-crown her unicorn and lead it forth at the advent of the New Age.

In a previous chapter, we stated that we are all involved in a world drama, in which the dragon, the Beast, is fighting furiously against a potential influx of limitless Love and Truth — the power of the Living Christ.

> *For we wrestle not against flesh and blood, but against princi-palities, against powers, against the rulers of the darkness of this world.*
>
> (*Ephesians, VI.* 12)

The Biblical prophesy applies to us today. Despite decanon-ization by Rome, St. George is still our patron saint. In legend, he is really less a dragon-slayer than a dragon-tamer. And the Beast, when overcome, is led through the streets by a virgin. This symbolism is beautifully conveyed by Uccello's painting, which depicts St. George pinning the dragon down with his lance, while the maiden stands meekly by, holding the beast with a silken leash. We may take the dragon to reflect the egoism arising from a materialistic world view. When the St. George in each of us has brought the beast under control, the virgin soul may lead it triumphantly through the marketplace. The allegory, then, embodies the task of modern man — to achieve the evolutionary step from egoism to true community. The unicorn's horn and St. George's lance are essentially the same principle.

As all great mythic figures reflect attributes and qualities of soul, we cannot neglect Arthur, that great enigma of British legend. Arthur too is a servant of the spirit. In legend, he sleeps with his knights beneath the hill, waiting until Britain shall need him again in battle, at which time he will come forth, "conquering and to conquer." Arthur is the champion of true Christianity against the powers of darkness, the traditional "defender of the faith." And for almost a millenium, there has been an obstinate and persistent belief that somehow he will indeed come again. On his tomb a prophetic inscription was carved:

HIC JACET ARTURUS REX QUONDAM
REXQUE FUTURUS
Here lies Arthur, the Once and Future King

Arthur, according to Blake, represents Albion, the archetypal quality in Britain's folk-soul. Thus he is a principle of true kingship, and embodies the virtues of justice and freedom. In this capacity, as a mythic figure, he cannot be debased by historical attempts to identify him with a fifth Century chieftain. On the contrary, he is a very real principle pervading the whole of British culture and its history. The "Matter of Britain," the predominant British myth, centers around a Golden Age in which man once lived, and which is destined to come again. In *Camelot and the Vision of Albion*, Geoffrey Ashe analyzes how this conviction runs like a silver thread through centuries of British reform movements. And now the passing of the Dark Age, the Kali Juga, is said in esoteric wisdom to precede the coming of a Golden Age when men will again walk with the beings of the spiritual worlds and find Shamballah, the blessed realm of the etheric.

And Michael and his angels overcame the Beast. And he laid hold on the dragon, that old serpent, which is the Devil and Satan, and bound him a thousand years. And cast him into the bottomless pit and shut him up and set a seal upon him, that he should deceive the nations no more till the thousand years should be fulfilled.

Michael's warrior representative, Arthur, after his long sojourn in the dark cave — perhaps the collective unconscious of the race — may indeed rise again, with royalty, within our hearts as champion of the New Age. We all live in a time when allegory speaks directly to us of what is transpiring on the subtler, invisible planes. Truth and the symbol hold good on many levels, and it is our loss if we choose to confine our thinking and interpretation solely to the provable and ponderable mundane — or the pedantic intellectual. So much more exists and calls to us. This is indeed an age of mystery, wonder and hope.

Let us close this book with the Great Invocation, which was

imparted to mankind from a high spiritual source in 1945. It expresses truths common to all the major religions, and is now being used across the world by people of many differing faiths and creeds. It is a prayer which focuses the call for help from man to the Higher Worlds. It admirably expresses the threefold nature of the Unity of Being, whether in man as a creature of thinking, feeling and will, or in a universe shot through with the Trinity of Divine Wisdom, Love and Power:

THE GREAT INVOCATION
From the point of Light within the Mind of God
Let Light stream forth into the minds of men.
Let Light descend on Earth.

From the point of Love within the Heart of God
Let Love stream forth into the hearts of men.
May Christ return to Earth.

From the center where the Will of God is known
Let purpose guide the little wills of men —
The purpose which the Masters know and serve.

From the center which we call the race of men
Let the Plan of Love and Light work out.
And may it seal the door where evil dwells.

Let Light and Love and Power restore the Plan on Earth.

About the Author

Sir George Trevelyan, BT., M.A., holds a vision of social renewal based on an inner willed change in personal consciousness. He has pioneered the teaching of spiritual knowledge as adult education in Great Britain and is one of our most respected teachers. He is aware that we are living in times of tremendous change in the material, psychic and spiritual level and that there is a kind of creative turmoil at work in the world which is a reflection of our innermost feelings as they strive to break through to a life of meaning and purpose. In 1971 he founded the Wrekin Trust, a charitable foundation which has become a focal point for many people who are committed to the exploration of their spiritual nature and the development of consciousness.